MW00626289

The Paradox of Having Your Sh*t Together

The Paradox of Having Your Sh*t Together
The Journey of Awakening Your Mind

Matthew W. Missimer

Published by Game Changer Publishing

Paperback ISBN: 978-1-963793-27-7
Hardcover ISBN: 978-1-963793-28-4
Digital: ISBN: 978-1-963793-29-1

www.GameChangerPublishing.com

This Book Is Dedicated to Mothers' Intuition

Thank you to my wife, Shannon. Your intuition leads our home on a daily basis as we raise our children. I am grateful for your leadership and for helping me to be the best father I can be. I love you and could not do this journey without your love, patience, and conviction for our life together, hand in hand.

Thank you, Mom, for being my guide and helping me through every phase of my journey. Your patience and compassion are unwavering, and I would not be the person I am today without your love, intuition, and mentorship.

Read This First

Just to say thanks for buying and reading my book, I would like to give you a few free bonus gifts, no strings attached!

The Paradox of Having Your Sh*t Together

The Journey of Awakening Your Mind

Matthew W. Missimer

www.GameChangerPublishing.com

Foreword by Mary Megan Stoneback, My Mom!

What does it mean to be a mother?

I was blessed with two healthy pregnancies and two beautiful children. Motherhood has been the focus of my life. My children share my heart, and truly, my destiny in life has been to raise my daughter and son and learn the lessons of love.

From the moment I knew I was pregnant, I became a protector and caregiver. The profound pleasure of nurturing and loving a child helped me understand the bond I shared with them. This bond enabled me to see and feel their greatest joys and their deepest moments of sadness. Seeing their eyes light up with excitement and living in their happiness brought incredible delights to me. The moments of sadness that are a part of our history were when we combined forces and grew. Empowered by instinct, the sacrifices I made came as naturally as breathing, and the rewards began to sketch the artwork of my life.

The power to love, care, and pray for my children every day throughout their lives has given a beautiful purpose to my life. The conversations we shared as they grew, their achievements, watching them fall in love, what an incredible volley of love. And today, I continue to see their trust in me and the beauty of our shared moments. I will be forever grateful for the lessons I have learned through their eyes.

What does it mean to be Matthew's mother?

Matthew, my heart is a magnificent reservoir of sweet memories and wonderful conversations. Your journey through life is a collage of some of the most beautiful moments of my life.

Raising a son had a small learning curve, and I embraced it fully. I was your first love, and I knew that would change and that every hug was to be cherished. Soon, I was to learn about your dreams, coupled with your adventurous spirit and how seriously you took action to achieve the goals you set for yourself. It has been inspiring to watch you focus your mind on something and accomplish it!

You are grown now, and the wonderful moments and memories continue. I feel your love in every hello and the simple title of mom, followed by a smile, warms my heart. I am incredibly grateful for that and for how much I am able to learn from you in our conversations. A pressure has been lifted to not always be the authority. I can relax and listen, as I often saw you do with me. Understanding how a man thinks is enlightening, but listening and learning from your son is extraordinary.

Matthew, you were so kind and thoughtful as a child, and you have carried those gifts throughout your life. Now I see a wonderful husband and father who loves his family abundantly, and I feel so blessed to be your mom. Thank you for helping me to understand that God has directed my every step, and I am exactly where I am meant to be. Thank you for being you and sharing your love and life with me.

Table of Contents

PART 1

Exploring the Paradoxes

CHAPTER 1

Vision Is Everything!

Today is July 9, 2085. It is my hundredth birthday. I am sitting on the deck of my refurbished sport fishing boat. The sun is coming up over the horizon, and I have a fresh cup of coffee in my favorite mug. Shannon is down below, sleeping peacefully.

My morning schedule has been the same now for 62 years. It is hard to believe that my mind, body, and soul have made it to this sunrise. I have been wishing myself a happy birthday every morning since February of 2023. Every day has been a gift. Every breath is cherished. I sit and reflect on what Shannon and I have done together, married for 73 years! It has been an epic journey exploring every feeling and emotion.

Personally, we have traveled the world with our children using every form of transportation. We did the RV life, the boats, trains, planes, and road trips. We have traveled to every continent and explored every spiritual practice firsthand. We cherished staying in The Motion of Gratitude®, which fueled our perspective.

We raised three beautiful children. Madelyn, Quinn, and Grayson have been our greatest teachers. They have mirrored back to us everything we needed to learn to be the very best we could. The five of us have been swimming against the current since 2020. We opened quite a can of worms that year. We have learned from each other how to live, love, and parent consciously every day since.

Professionally, the journey to running a multinational company focused on building a community around gratitude has been so much fun. When we started the vision in 2017, most people could not grasp what we were up to. Some days, we forgot, too!

The six-year cocoon process led to an incredible butterfly in 2024. That was the year our entire life changed. Shannon and I built a company hand in hand, one that teaches people that gratitude is the gateway and destination of the healing journey. Gratosis® became a board-certified positive diagnosis, and the medical industry began chasing it.

It took time to build momentum, but once it started, it could not be stopped. I am grateful that we built an organization that has had a measurable impact on mental health around the world. We started at home by creating a beautiful life for our children, and that inspired us to help people pull up when they were going "through the motions."

Financially, we took a lot of risks early on in life. In my 20s and 30s, I lived for the money game. I learned to play, and it almost destroyed me. It is not that money is bad, but it was my primary motivation from 12 to 33. It took me four years to learn that the money game does not make you happy.

Coming into a large sum of money at age 33 changed the trajectory of my life, but I am beyond grateful for my financial planning career of 18 years. It taught me everything I needed to know about the money game.

When I was 37, I started playing the human game full time. Since February 24, 2023, I have taken time for myself first thing every morning. Doing so has helped me become the man I am today.

My wife and I built a company to provide wealth for every family member, and we did it by focusing on mastering our human experience. We stay grateful and present in the moment. We lead with love and kindness in every decision. Living in Gratosis has afforded us the life to Feel the Impact® of an intentional gratitude practice. Through this belief system, we have been able to provide for our family for generations to come.

As I finish my cup of coffee and listen to my favorite music, tears come to my eyes. I did it! I lived, loved, and parented consciously. I played hard and have the happiness to show for it. I love life. I am ready to go home when God calls me. Until that last breath, I will continue to wake up and watch the sun come up. I thank myself, God, and my family for this day. I say happy birthday to myself. Every day is a celebration of my life. I smile! I am Gratosis.

CHAPTER 2

The Quest for Cool "Stuff"

When I was 12 years old, I wanted to be on every boat bigger than my grandfather's 24-foot Grady-White—"Pop Pop's toy." I would watch in awe as beautiful boats went by. What do these people do? How can they afford this? I want that. This ignored the fact that I was safely floating on my grandfather's boat in the vast, unforgivable ocean. This was the beginning of my material desires. Getting a 24-foot boat at 12 is not a rational starting point. Let's start with the nicest soccer cleats on the market.

When I was 16, my dad bought me a Ford Thunderbird. Free was a good price, but now I needed a car that cost $1. Better yet, the "cool kids" had Jeep Wranglers. I needed to work hard and save up so I could be a "cool kid," too. If I could save $7,500 to buy a Jeep with my own money and hard work, that meant I could "keep up."

A little note on my parents. My dad was one of four, and my mom was one of seven. My dad's family worked hard and built things with their hands. I look up to the men on my dad's side of the family, and I am grateful for the genes I got from them that gave me grit. My mom was from a large family, with the oldest benefiting from higher education, but the younger you were, the harder your family position worked against you. My mom taught me that feelings are good. They are meant to be had, and we should respect others while they are having them. I cannot imagine having that many children. Three is the perfect number for Shannon and me!

My parents had my older sister at a young age, setting in motion the miracle of my life. The timing for my arrival might not have been perfect for them, but I am grateful for the chain of events that led to the miracle of my life. Two children and six grandchildren keep everyone on their toes!

The journey through high school was enjoyable, but it does not stand out as a defining moment or collection of years. I saw it as a means to an end that would bleed over into the next chapter of my life. Perhaps that is a theme when it comes to my education. I have always seen the value of education, and I see it for my kids today. What stood out the most, though, was the necessity of education. At a young age, I noticed the importance of that piece of paper, the high school or college diploma. This piece of paper required effort, but once attained, it did not have to be maintained. Kinda cool.

You work hard in high school, and you get a GPA and a diploma. If your GPA is good, you will progress to the next opportunity to get another diploma. You never look back and say, "I must do [X] or [Y] to keep this diploma." What is done is done. Sacrificing now to complete the education leads to a perpetual benefit. That was a no-brainer for me. Education has been a cornerstone of my progression, and I believe there is an unspoken game to it, which I will share. I am not saying it is good or bad; I am simply sharing the viewpoint I explored as a 17-year-old.

This accidental lesson was very valuable in my young adulthood. The game of "stuff" has complicated problems and benefits. The problems of keeping up with the Joneses are well known. The benefits, however, are rarely discussed. The upward spiral of wanting more, working harder, wanting more… you get the point. It works if your measuring stick is getting cool stuff.

"More better" in the college admissions game was a serious level-up from the Jeep Wrangler. The Jeep was $7,500. Now, I was looking at schools that cost $15,000 to $35,000 a year. The stakes were increasing, but in my simple calculation, the outcomes were easy to measure. I noticed that people who paid more for school obsessed more about the piece of paper. This makes sense. The more you pay for something, the more likely you are to make a big deal about it.

My mom and stepdad had offered to pay for state school. That could have been an easier road because I would have graduated debt-free. Instead, I opted to go to St Joseph's University in Philadelphia. *"The Hawk Will Never Die."* This was never my mantra, but I am happy for the culture it created and that I got to be a part of.

This "more better" decision was a scary one. A couple of factors needed to be in order. First, I had to trust my gut about what private college to attend. I had narrowed it down to two. When I walked the SJU campus, it felt right. I think we can often overthink things and ignore this feeling. If something feels right, I find, more often than not, it is right. Second, I had to bet on myself. I had to believe that I could succeed at a level that would justify the expense and allow me to pay off the $75,000 of debt I would incur. Third, I had to lean on my mom and stepdad for support. This meant two things: they believed in me and saw something in me that allowed them to encourage me to go down this path, but they also had to cosign my debt.

College felt like the big leagues. I would later learn it was just the beginning of scaling up, but as a 19-year-old, it felt heavy. I applied early, with SJU as Plan A and a great state school as Plan B. I still remember the day I got my acceptance letter. It was Thanksgiving weekend. Everyone said, "Little envelope bad. Big envelope, you are in." I opened the mailbox and found a letter from SJU.

The envelope was small, and my disappointment could not have been more obvious. I walked down the driveway back to the house to open the letter with my mom. I guess I needed emotional support rather than a private rejection by the mailbox. Or maybe I did not want the neighbors to see me crying. I do not remember my thought process as rejection seized control of my psyche.

When I opened the letter and it said, "Congratulations," I remember feeling pure joy. Dare I say, I felt Gratosis. I could not believe I had gotten in. My sister was the first to go to college on my dad's side, and now I was number two. Not only was I going to college, but I'd gotten into a school that people in our area saw as a great way to be in the know and keep up.

It is amazing how little energy went into fear of paying back the money I would have to borrow for my education. The value of attending this university far outweighed the cost. This was the beginning of my understanding that cost is only an issue in the absence of value. My mom wrote the deposit check the next day, and I accepted my spot in my next adventure.

College was everything I thought it would be. After a few semesters, I quickly adopted the same mindset I had in high school. This journey was a means to an end. Don't get me wrong. I had a great time and learned a lot from this adventure, but I saw how finite this time would be and how important it was to level up in my next game: the workforce.

Before moving on, I want to share a couple of lessons that forever changed the trajectory of my life. The first is the 80/20 rule—The Pareto Principle. The Pareto Principle suggests that 80% of effects come from 20% of causes, highlighting the importance of focusing on the most productive inputs for the best outcomes. Traditionally, this applies to client service, but in college, I was struck by a different insight: do the opposite of what 80% of the people around you are doing. We are pack animals, and I find we tend to conform to the crowd, following the path of least resistance. I do this all the time!

What I have found, though, is that there are key moments and circumstances when you want to be the 20%. For example, It is not cool to raise your hand in class to answer a question. I found this to be an ideal situation to do the opposite of the rest of the crowd. And now that I have spoken in front of many audiences, I understand this truth even better. The professor is up there, giving their all to teach students something valuable, but the audience usually gives very little in return. It can be lonely up there.

When I engaged with professors, they engaged with me, and I did better both inside and outside the classroom. The law of reciprocity was introduced into my life in an intentional manner. In high school, I got the president's award in the yearbook. I had my own hall pass, which let me exit the classroom for a large part of the day.

In high school, my behavior was subconscious. In college, I learned to do this consciously. My intentions were always pure, and the outcome was positive. I believed that if I put extra effort into having a relationship with professors and going above and beyond in the classroom, it would lead to better grades. True or false, this was an important part of keeping my GPA high in college.

I believe that education is an incredible leveling-up tool, but the student has to engage. The more I engaged, the easier class got. I received better grades because I learned the more I cared, the more professors cared about me. The law of reciprocity is almost unavoidable.

Next up, work. With my work history and income, the credit card companies thought I was mature enough to sign on the dotted line. Sign up here, and you can buy $2,000 worth of stuff you can't afford right now, but you can afford later. When you buy that stuff, we will charge you $40/month in interest, but you only have to pay $50/month. You will never pay the debt off if that is your plan. Not to worry; you have your STUFF now.

At the age of 33, I reached the peak of the keeping-up game, and it forever changed my life. I made a professional move that allowed my 12-year-old self to fulfill a dream. I had come to a crossroads in my professional journey, a tipping point that forced me to look for another company to do business with. I received a large sum of money to help with the transition. I was choosing to become an employee financial advisor. I wanted to try a different avenue in the industry after 15 years.

This was a very scary moment. I attached the dream of owning a boat to the transition. I researched the boat I wanted and picked out a Pursuit OS385. This was a boat I dreamed of having as a boy. It had three engines, air conditioning, a full galley, and enough room for my family of five to sleep on it.

I have always backed myself into situations to force myself to follow through. Good or bad, it has always worked! In this situation, the week before I transitioned to my new company, I put a $50,000 non-refundable deposit down on the boat. I only had $60,000 in my checking account, so I needed to make the transition now. And so, three weeks later, I took delivery of the largest material dream I have ever had!

I wish the story had a happy ending, but this was the beginning of a very confusing chapter in my life. Very quickly, Shannon and I realized we were not on the same page with this adventure. The kids were four, 18 months, and five months old. Everything about a day on the water was stressful. It was simply too soon to have this hobby in my life. This was the first time in our marriage that *my* dream was disrupting the flow of *our* dream.

Every time I used the boat, feelings came up for both of us. Shannon wanted to support me, but fishing and boating are time-intensive hobbies. I would use the boat as professional entertainment to justify the time away. This did not solve the fact that three months out of the year, I was sleeping on the boat two nights a week to go out into the middle of the ocean to sometimes catch fish. Do not get me wrong, I had incredible memories on that boat, *Gratosis*. In the end, my *Gratosis* was disrupting our family Gratosis.

In the fall of 2021, after only two seasons on the boat, I realized this was not the right time to own this boat. It came to light in a very abrupt way. I was taking the boat out by myself for the last ride of the season. I had forced the whole situation, squeezing it into my schedule. I left the dock knowing the tide was not right. The whole situation was set up for problems. I left the inlet, heading into the ocean, knowing that this might be the last time I used the boat.

On the way back, I was coming down the channel, and the tide had gone fully out. I cut the corner a little too tightly, and I went from 30 knots to zero in a couple hundred feet. And there I was, sitting on sand in the middle of the bay. A situation that I had snuck into my schedule was now going to require a four-hour wait for the tide to come back up.

At first, I felt frustration and anger. All I wanted to do was enjoy one last ride on my boat before the marina winterized it. I also felt that this chapter in my life was coming to a close, and I had thought that taking the boat out one more time would be a good way to complete it. I might have yelled. I was totally "tapped out." My mind was all over the place, and all I wanted to do was freak out.

Fortunately, I was using the tools of meditation and journaling. I sat down and meditated for 15 minutes. Then I took my phone out and started writing parts of the book you are currently reading. I took a frustrating moment and turned it into a moment of clarity. This moment was my sign that the boat chapter was closing. I was forcing everything about it, and it was not providing joy for me or my family. It was time to surrender and let go of the idea of the dream.

Do you have any dreams in your life that you will do anything to achieve? Are you doing anything today that is only for your benefit but is jeopardizing your relationships? In hindsight, that was never my intention. Quite the opposite. I thought our family of five was going to do amazing things on the boat and build memories. I hadn't been able to calculate the unintended consequences of owning the boat. I had been too obsessed with my dream to realize it could contradict my family's dream.

Shannon was beyond supportive during this two-year chapter with the boat. Her patience was insane. The best part of this story is that I put the boat up for sale, and it did not sell. I told my broker to take the boat off the market because it was not worth losing money. Thirty days later, he called and said the marina would buy it from me. I sold the boat and walked away with roughly the same amount I had put down. There was plenty of cost along the way, but this was a pretty happy ending financially. If you have owned a boat, this may sound like a miracle.

Have you accomplished a dream that is currently not bringing you the joy you thought it would? Does your ego know what to do with this paradox? I have always been fascinated by the mind's inability to let go of something we thought we wanted. There is so much power in saying goodbye to things that are no longer serving you.

People around you will be confused when you change course like this. Your ego will want justification for why you changed course. What will people think? I had to explore all these thoughts. I had been talking about this dream since I had written my first vision in 2008. I had done it! I had bought my dream, and now I was selling my dream.

It takes courage to close doors. Do you have anything in your life right now that is not bringing you joy? If so, get a piece of paper and a pen and write, "I am grateful for…" finishing the sentence with the item in question (for example, "I am grateful for my boat"). Then, list everything you can think of that makes you grateful for it. Once you have written it all down, ask yourself: Will this continue to make me grateful moving forward? Have I gotten joy from this thing? Is it worth having anymore? Is my intuition telling me that it is no longer serving me?

If you conclude that 1) you are grateful for this thing, 2) the thing no longer serves you, and 3) your intuition knows it is time to pivot, then make the choice to move on. The creative solution will present itself if you are grateful for the dream! This will be the easiest pivot I will share. Material things can be bought and sold. You may lose money, but that is easier to justify than what comes next.

Let's tie in the first part of the book, the vision I wrote for my hundredth birthday, and discuss how that could apply to the quest for cool stuff. Writing a vision is one of the most critical parts of the pursuit of your happiness, what I call Gratosis. I wrote my first vision in 2008. When I reflect on that vision, it was very centered around materialism. I was a young, single professional. One of my major focuses, which you've read about in this chapter, was buying a boat. Thousands of actions had to take place for me to accomplish this goal.

Fast forward to the paradox that played out in my quest for cool stuff. I had chased the boat, and I had gotten it, and then I had realized that it wasn't fulfilling me in the way that I thought it would. So, what are the things you have in your life that you've dreamed of for years? What are the actions and behaviors you're doing daily to pursue them? Are you neglecting or leaving out parts of your life in that pursuit, and is that causing resentment anywhere in your life? If it is, check in with yourself and talk to the people who are closest to you. The timing might not be right.

If you already have "the thing" and it is messing with another part of your life, it is time to make a change. I justified having the boat because I had a ton of fun with it, and I got to use my professional life to validate my hobby. In the end, this dream did not align with my circumstances. It was creating a hard time for my wife because she needed me to be around more. Also, I was out doing my thing and leaving her alone with the hardest job.

I was doing all of these things for other people that required focus and time. I would get the boat ready, people would show up around midnight, and we would head out into the ocean. Then we would fish all day and have a lot of fun. When we returned to the dock, all those people would go home. I would clean up the boat, spend the night on it, and then wake up the next morning and be home before the kids woke up. This process was really fun for me but also tiring.

I realized that this thing that I had put on a pedestal for 20 years had become a vice. It was pulling me away from where I needed to be. This truth was hard for me to wrap my head around. Is there a thing that you thought was everything you ever wanted, but it's creating more problems than solutions for you? Admitting this is the first step to fixing the situation! Recognize that you have a problem. This thing might be pulling you away from your family, or maybe it's preventing you from doing the work you need to do to continue to move towards your future successes, whatever they may be.

This is the paradox that I had to run into head first because it didn't make sense to me. I wanted the object of my desire to be everything I thought it would be. Instead, the result ended up being the opposite.

Leading with gratitude means acknowledging the beauty of what you've done. Then you can realistically assess what it's not currently doing. Your intuition will help you with this part of the process, telling you all the reasons why you need to make this pivot. Once you do this exercise, if you conclude that you are grateful for the journey but that it's no longer a part of where you're supposed to be, then your brain will instantly lock into a creative solution.

It is very easy to pivot away from things because they are material items. Hopefully, they are worth something, so you're able to sell them. If not, then give them away or leave the environment that no longer serves you.

The hardest thing for the human brain to wrap its head around is sunk cost. I learned this all through my financial career with investments. Sometimes, things do not work out, and we have to walk away. If it is a circumstance where you're losing money, ask yourself, will keeping this thing make me happy? No? You have to wrap your head around that loss. If you do, I promise that the headspace you free up will more than compensate for what you've let go, and you'll forget about the money part of the equation.

CHAPTER 3

The Professional Keeping-Up Game

I was a financial planner. As you can imagine, when your entire day revolves around money, it tends to bleed into your behaviors and thoughts. Some people have a hard time talking about money. For me, it was part of life. I had zero feelings about how much money people have or what they spend it on. This raises an interesting question: if I did not care, why did I spend so much energy making sure others knew I had a lot of money?

There is a common thought in my industry. People need to see you are doing well so they can see you have the "secret" to success to share with them. I fell headfirst into this trap, and the "fake it until you make it" journey became pretty intense in my life. I was also comparing myself to other professionals in the office. Never mind that I was 21 years old, with $80,000 in student loan debt, while they were in their late 40s and 50s. At the time, my brain refused to register the vast difference in our circumstances.

I am sure you can guess where this one is going. I sold the Jeep Wrangler. Wearing a suit every day with no air conditioning can be a problem. I could not afford a new car yet because I was working on one hundred percent commission. Thank you, big sister, for lending me your car for six months until I could save up!

In the saving-up time, I relived my 16-year-old pattern: work hard and save. This time, I was obsessed with buying a certified, pre-owned Lexus IS350, with a price of around $28,000 and navy blue, of course! I would visit the Lexus dealership on a weekly basis. Sometimes, I would do a drive-by, and other times, I'd take one out for a test drive with a familiar salesperson who worked hard to sell me that car.

I remember the day I bought it. It was a little different this time because I put $5,000 down through a wire. I was growing up, no cash in hand. The payment was higher, but I was building confidence in my sales. Never mind that I had those student loans on a six-month deferment. Looking back, I see how caught up I was in showing people I was doing well.

Meanwhile, I struggled every month to pay my bills. This was the paradox playing out. I was showing people that I was doing well, but at the same time, I was living in fear.

I conditioned myself to get very good at living in fear. From the outside looking in, I was an excellent salesperson. I was winning all the awards, and the external brand was in great order. Meanwhile, I was breaking slowly inside. I had many coping mechanisms for this. One was to ignore the situation. This was a revenue problem, not an expense problem. Two, I told myself that everyone else around me had nice things, so I should, too, because I wanted clients to see me doing well so I would attract more of them. Three, I was having fun and living in the extremes on the weekends. I had to decompress.

I remained stuck in this pattern for 13 years. People challenged me on many interesting behaviors: buying new cars, taking crazy vacations, and exploring crazy ideas. All of these actions were symptoms of a deeper truth. I had become addicted to backing myself into corners and selling my way out of them. The external professional reward was recognition by my company and peers. The external personal reward was stuff: fine suits, nice watches, cool cars. You name it, I was chasing it.

No matter what I acquired, though, it was always fleeting. I look back at the stuff, and I couldn't care less. It simply does not stand out in my mind as relevant. But when I look back at the trips and adventures, I loved them. This was a big lesson and continues to be a theme in my life. Don't get me wrong; I like having nice things, but my real joy comes from experiences. I can be selectively cheap with physical items, but I can justify just about any expense when it comes to a good adventure.

I can share stories for pages about the things I did to portray a brand to others. I am sure you get the point, though. We have all been told that money does not buy us happiness. I agree, but I would take it in another direction. Money does not buy us happiness if we spend it on things that do not make us happy and pretend like we are. I can honestly say I knew I was living out a broken pattern, but it was so normal around me that I thought this was the way most people lived. It was not until age 34 that I figured out how wrong I was, but I will get there later.

"The paradox of having your sh*t together" is very prevalent in this part of my life. Everyone thought I was doing great, but inside, I was questioning many of my decisions. My default setting was to follow the pack. I was living out the opposite of the 80/20 desires I had learned in college. The benefits were great, however, because I was in a highly productive work culture. It taught me a skill that I will carry with me for the rest of my life. I learned to sell myself, and I learned to make money. I just needed to hire a brand manager for my mind, so I was happy with who I was. I am grateful that I found someone to help me figure this one out!

Are you faking it until you make it? Does your passion align with your soul mission? I have zero judgment if your answer is no. This was a very important lily pad in my journey. I wish someone would have taught me another way sooner. I was in a work culture where this behavior was normalized. I had no perspective on another way. Looking back, there were several red flags:

1. Buying things that made me look successful but that I could not afford.
2. Selling products with an agenda to make a commission. I knew I was helping people, AND I was good at helping them come to my desired outcome.
3. Losing sleep at night trying to figure out how I was going to pay my employees. Scaling too fast, so other people thought I required a team because I was SO busy.
4. Letting loose on a Friday night because I needed to unwind from the week.
5. Going into credit card debt to wear suits and portray a brand that I had not earned.

We are walking a fine line here. Please do not confuse this kind of debt with investing in yourself. I have done that plenty of times. I have hired many coaches using credit cards. I know this was a good use of debt, and it always paid for itself. I am focused on the materialistic side of the equation at this juncture.

If you are doing anything like the points above, first, forgive yourself. I am sure this behavior is a product of your environment, and your ego is enjoying part of this evolution of yourself. Then ask yourself, *If a video camera were following me around, would my actions prove that I have earned my current circumstance?*

This is a scary question. I have asked myself this question thousands of times. Sometimes, the answer is yes, and sometimes, it's no. Whenever I hear "no," I ask, "Am I faking it?" There is no reason for you to share your answer with the world. If your answer is yes, write down all the behaviors you are doing on a day-to-day basis. Look in the mirror and stare into your own eyes. Ask yourself, "Do I want to keep pretending that I have earned this current situation?" This is a raw exercise, and I encourage you to be gentle. Once you have taken this moment, write everything down, and then find someone you love and ask them for help. Accountability and processing are the only ways through this muddy thought process. You might feel like your mind is stuck in honey. Welcome to the first step of doing work to align your situation with yourself!

Before I jump into the teaching side of this, I wanted to share that culture is a critical part of the professional walk. I firmly believe that whoever you surround yourself with and whatever you read is who you become. So, I want to put an asterisk on this part of my story because my culture caused part of this evolution as well. Financial advisors are in a culture of acquiring, where young advisors fake it until they make it.

I had grown up without a lot of money, and this was my first experience with the professional world. I remember when I started my internship, I had to call my mom to say, "Hey, Mom. I need to get a suit." We went to Macy's and got my first suit so I could get ready for the interview. I was walking into an entirely new world with a new costume and persona. I had to build something so foreign to me, and the only resources I had were the people around me. In hindsight, I saw the life that these men and women in their 40s and 50s had, and I wanted it. It all makes sense, but that does not mean it did not take a toll on me.

I am grateful for that culture because, without it, I would never have thrived or built the life that I have. Now, I am at the point where I can recognize what was good for me then is not necessarily good for me now. Use the story of my red flags to identify ones in your current life experience.

First, I bought many things at the beginning of my career to show people that I was very successful when I had not earned that level of success. I'll use an easy example. I was 23 years old, and I bought a Mercedes. I had closed a couple of good deals, and I had a good bit of money in the bank. In many families, the car you drive is a sign of your success. It is an external representation that everyone can see. I took this one a little too far! I was way ahead of myself in terms of what I had earned. I figured this out about three or four months into owning the car. People would say things to me or make comments that made me feel insecure that I was even driving it. The car payment was huge, which created a double-edged sword. I had put myself in a situation where I had to sell more things to make the car payment. This was all in an effort to keep up with the people around me, and those people were sometimes 10 to 15 years older than me.

Now, you might say, "Why didn't you understand this as a 24-year-old?" My behavior was very common in the company that I was working with. I was in my own little bubble of normalizing behaviors like this. Is there anything in your life where you're normalizing a behavior to keep up with your professional environment? You might be walking into a paradox that you probably want to unwind.

I was a sales professional and financial advisor, selling insurance, annuities, and investment platforms. I had to go out on a daily basis to either see more people or sell more stuff. Those were the only two outcomes that would provide for the persona I had built. If you are in a sales career but are putting your agenda first, you have to look in the mirror and say, "Why am I putting my agenda first?" I was still selling products that the people that I was serving needed, but the cadence and speed had unavoidable, unintended consequences.

What I've observed with many sales professionals is that seeing more people and creating more opportunities creates more work. More work equals more rejection. Over time, all humans will seek more pleasure and less pain.

This leads sales professionals to see the same amount of people while becoming more creative in what they sell.

Sometimes, though, that creative behavior can be at odds with the client's desired outcome. The advisor might think that they can help a client by selling them a product with a higher commission and, therefore, it's a win-win if they're getting a good product. This is a slippery slope of justification. Any financial product with a high commission is designed to be sold. If everyone bought it, they would not have to pay salespeople a lot to sell it. You have to second-guess that behavior because it's highly likely that the products you're selling are not in alignment with their desires. Absorbing this truth is both humbling and frustrating. I believe all sales professionals have run into this quandary at some point in their careers.

Are you building a life right now that keeps you up at night? Are you waking up between two and four in the morning, and your cortisol levels are going through the roof? Do you want to jump out of bed and run from a lion because you're so scared that what you've created is not sustainable? This pattern was so prevalent in my life. I would go to bed at 10 o'clock and wake up at three in the morning. Fear and urgency were my default settings. I would try to go back to sleep, to no avail.

There are plenty of productive things to do at this time of day before the world starts moving. I wasn't doing them. Instead, I was scrolling through the internet, procrastinating, and avoiding facing my truth. I still wake up early some days, and I journal, meditate, and do things for my own self-care and love. But this is a different type of mental state from my past. Now I know that if I'm not sleeping, I have a scaling and cadence issue. I am human. I fall back into my old familiar all the time. Now I am faster to react. If you're scaling too fast or running too fast, and you're increasing the cortisol levels in your body so much that you're in fight-or-flight mode all the time, you will not be able to make conscious, meaningful choices on a daily basis that will be aligned with your purpose.

There's an old saying: "You have to slow down to speed up." So, if you find yourself in a poor sleep pattern, instead of saying, "I am going to embrace this fierceness inside of me and adopt a warrior mentality," take a step back and acknowledge that we live in a beautiful time in history where you don't have to be that type of warrior. Instead, adopt a self-love mindset and focus on creating a healthy sleep pattern.

I'm not telling everyone they have to go to bed at nine o'clock and wake up at five o'clock in the morning. Everyone has their own sleep cadence. What I'm working to impress upon you is that healthy sleep is critical for an abundant mindset. There's a reason that the number one method of torture is depriving someone of sleep. If you have children, you know that the first year of life, when the child is not sleeping through the night, can be one of the hardest times of your life. One of the foundations of a happy, healthy life is developing a consistent sleep pattern.

When I was in this state, I would live for the weekend. *Weekend energy*: "I've worked so hard for the last five days that I've earned the right to cut loose or unwind." I did this for years. I would work 60-hour weeks and, during the week, go to happy hours for entertainment. I was in the financial industry, mentoring and coaching young advisors. Entertainment was a critical part of keeping up the image of "We're all doing really well." Meanwhile, as you can imagine, a lot of these young advisors, including myself at the time, were secretly or quietly falling apart inside.

On Fridays, I would work till about three o'clock, and then I had earned the right to go out to a nice meal, have a couple of drinks, and numb myself. Saturday would come, and we would party, day drink—you name it. Then, Sunday: fun day. Cycles like that, five days on, two days off, create an unhealthy mental state.

I'm grateful for this part of my waking-up process to be a father. With one child, I could still keep up this persona. My reality was when Madelyn (my oldest) was born, I would still work 60 hours a week and would only be a dad on the weekends. I would leave for work at 5 a.m., and I would get home after she was in bed. At the time, I felt that this "sacrifice" was necessary, but was it? I don't know. Perhaps NOT in hindsight. That was part of me keeping up the game.

Then, when my second child, Quinn, came along, I needed to be around more. I cut my work schedule to two nights a week and was always home on the weekends, though I still kept up the weekend drinking. Then our third, Grayson, came, and it became so difficult for me to be grumpy at all on the weekends that it was impossible for me to keep up my weekend behavior. This is when I had to confront the reality that I was using alcohol to unwind from all the winding up.

If you find yourself winding up on a daily basis and then requiring a tool to unwind on the weekend, you have to look at yourself in the mirror and say, "Is this a healthy pattern? Is this serving me and my family?" I'm grateful I have a super-cool wife. Shannon always supports me when I'm in these patterns. We all have our things. That is the beauty of being in a relationship with someone who is cheering for you and not against you. We had to address her need for me to be more present in our family unit. Communication was critical for us to resolve this cycle.

I would also turn into a fun dad. I would have a couple of beers in my unwinding effort, which would also unwind the discipline Shannon had put into the children over the last five days. This was eye-opening for me. I had no idea, and it was not in my psyche. Not only was I creating a pattern that was hurting myself, but the unintended consequence was that I was hurting Shannon's rhythm with our children. We no longer do weekend energy. I say that every Friday. "No weekend energy." We treat Saturday and Sunday the same way we treat every other day of the week.

Alcohol is no longer part of my journey. I don't judge anyone who drinks alcohol; whatever your tools are, more power to you. But for me, every weekend, I wake up at the same time as the rest of the week. I still meditate at the same time. I write in my gratitude journal. I look at my schedule and prioritize the things that need to be done. Saturdays and Sundays are all about self-care, self-love, and family.

Shannon and I each get two hours of quiet time each day, Saturday and Sunday, whether that's yoga, breathwork, or taking ourselves out to lunch. While one of us is having quiet time, the other takes care of the three kids. Then, by two o'clock on Saturday and Sunday, it's family time. We love nature. When we're in Costa Rica, we go to the beach. In Utah, we go hiking. We find ways to be out in nature as a family. It's also critical that we eat together. For a family of five with little kids, that involves cooking. These are the mindset shifts that we require to avoid some of those traps of weakened-energy behavior.

Last topic: credit. I deeply believe in my heart and my mind that we have to invest in ourselves. We need to bet on what is to come for us. The best investment we can make is in our own development, and sometimes, this requires debt. I've done this plenty of times.

The credit card debt that I'm referring to here is using credit to buy things to create the persona externally, not internally. I would spend a lot of money on wearing fancy suits and shoes that everyone wanted. I would wear watches that I thought defined me, and I had become a materialistic version of myself. This version was never fully aligned with my true self, but I thought I needed to live like that to show the world that I had done really well for myself. But at the same time, I didn't own it.

Selling my business and paying off all the debt was a wake-up call. I looked at the things that I was wearing, and I didn't want to wear them anymore. Now I had money in the bank, and I had my liquidation event at 33. I stopped wearing my Rolex. I stopped wearing suits. I stopped wearing fancy shoes, and my self-image became the purest version of me because I was no longer putting myself out there to the world in an attempt to gain something. This was the most profound moment for me.

Today, my outfit of choice is yoga clothes. I don't think about what people think of my clothing or what it costs. And every time I put my clothes on, I ask myself, *Is this comfortable? Do I feel good about myself?* The credit card debt that I used to create this false persona became such a comedy in hindsight. Look at your credit card statements, look at your debt, and ask yourself, *Is this debt portraying a brand that is in line with my soul's mission?* If that answer is no, laugh at yourself.

Put together a plan to pay off the debt. Put together a strategy to move forward. Be grateful for what you've done and stop doing it. And reflect on the exercise we talked about in the last chapter.

CHAPTER 4

One Person Can Change Everything

I met Shannon in the winter of 2010. We were both in relationships at the time, so we engaged in the typical service-level introduction: Nice to meet you. Where are you from? Do you have any siblings? I really like that we started here because neither of us had an agenda in the beginning. We were friends, and it was simple—until it was not. As our relationship evolved, we knew there was more. We also knew that our current relationships were not the right fit. Getting to know one another proved to us that there could be more to this than we were currently getting, regardless of whether it was with each other.

Fortunately for me, it was with each other. Shannon's childhood was very different from mine. The details are not relevant, but the fact that we came from very different circumstances created a healthy perspective for both of us.

There is one story that defines the beginning of our journey and her viewpoint on the materialism that I was living. I had made a mistake on my taxes, and I owed quite a bit. I asked the firm if I could borrow money, and my mentor at the time said I had to scale down my brand. I had overextended myself and bought a Mercedes E350 coupe. Awesome car! But it was a bad idea for a 24-year-old to be driving it. I took the perception of reality too far on this one.

The deal was that if I sold the car and got a less expensive one, the firm would give me the loan. I was very grateful for this lesson and to the firm for doing this. As you can imagine, it was not a productive day for my ego. I went to the Mercedes dealership and traded in my 10-month-old car that I had put a substantial down payment on. You can imagine this math did not work in my favor. I traded it in for a Mercedes C300. I know some of you are thinking, "You poor thing." I agree now, but at the time, I was feeling pretty bad for myself.

Shannon did not feel bad for me, though. I called her to tell her what had happened, and you would have thought I had won the lottery. I was embarrassed and defeated, and she turned it into an amazing transaction. She only saw the good in the situation. She pointed out all the reasons this was a good idea and how much she loved the car. At that moment, I learned one of the most amazing lessons when it came to what she cared about. It was definitely not my stuff! This is one example of this shift in mindset among thousands. It is easy to pinpoint and speaks to a part of my life that was ready to change, and I needed it.

Shannon and I started dating, and we were on the "no-plan plan." I think that lasted two weeks. It is amazing how one person can change everything. This was the beginning of me redefining what a healthy relationship is. Through strengthening our relationship, I began to question everything. This was not an overnight process. My definition of success changed much faster than my professional or financial. It was like I was safe at home and still put on a costume to go to work. I was entirely different around clients and coworkers than I was with Shannon. This duality was exhausting, and I was fortunate that Shannon let me decompress and listened to all the contradictions in my mind. Her patience is beyond my comprehension, and this shines so brightly as she teaches our three children her life lessons.

Shannon and I still got caught up in the keeping up, but it started to drift from my identity. Where it continued to show up was in big purchases. The stakes were higher now as we bought our first house and then moved to our next. I bought a Range Rover and Land Rover for Shannon on the same day, and we lived in a house that we only used half of. I bought that boat I mentioned in a previous chapter. I share these facts because, in my mind, I had reached the peak of the climb. It looked like we had everything, but we were still missing something. My analogy is that we were chasing a unicorn up a mountain. When we got to the top, there was no unicorn and a higher mountain on the other side. We knew something had to change.

Just as we did at the beginning of our courtship, we changed *personally* before we did professionally or financially. From many people's perspectives, it looked like we were making fast moves because our external life changed in what seemed like a flash. Selling our house after living there for two years and moving four miles away is an example of that. In reality, we had been changing personally for quite some time. We were figuring out what made us happy. Having two kids at this point expedited our growing up. They made us question ourselves every day. The internal changes started to become clear, and our external changes followed.

What makes us happy? What do we want to teach our children? These were big questions that I could not find an answer to. Up to this point, I had always chased money and stuff. I thought this made me happy. I know now it was creating a cycle: success, fear, acquisition, fear, success, acquisition, and on and on I went. What Shannon and I figured out is that we had to redefine success. It became clear over many conversations and glasses of wine. We nailed down a couple of themes. It's important to focus on themes rather than outcomes. If you track outcomes, you are goal-setting, and there is a potential to fall into the trap of acquiring things.

Our themes were general, but they allowed us to move forward and update our definitions of success. Here they are, in no particular order. The first was adventure or travel. We believe that travel fuels our perspective of the world. It makes us feel alive and creative. We love planning adventures! I believe I like the planning process more than the destination. This would play out in a big way in the coming years. The second is nature. We crave the outdoors and green space. We do not have to be in a national park. We need to see trees and be outside in the sun. The third is gratitude. We found that the more grateful we were, the less we needed. This did not mean we stopped having a vision for what was next. It meant we stopped living in the future all the time.

My chase obsession started to subside. This opened a new door in my mind. I was on the other side and did not know how I could go back. This was when we started to break down the paradox and have our sh*t. We started getting vulnerable and letting people in. We shared more about what we wanted and why with the people who cared about us. I wanted people to know that everything was not okay. I shared my views, and I stopped agreeing with everyone just because it was part of the deal. It felt like we were fish swimming upstream. Some days, it felt like a river at flood stage. Through this evolution, we changed everything!

Shannon and I have explored a lot of different healing modalities and paths to our spiritual evolution. There are times when she leads and times when I do. We have daily practices to stay connected to our inner voices. They are similar and also very different. We have found the most important part of our relationship is communication. The last four years of being nomads have required relentless patience and constant communication. Without them, we would definitely be "going through the motions"! We are meant to live in companionship with abundance. I firmly believe the universe has our backs in those two respects.

Are you in a relationship that lacks communication? Do you find yourself bickering more than communicating? Gratitude is the gateway to the healing journey. When Shannon and I are in a tough spot, we will talk about it to one another. It is impossible to be grateful for someone and mad at them at the same time.

If you are in a time of change or going through the motions with your significant other, take a step back. The answer is right in front of you. You owe it to yourself to turn towards that person and do the work. If the person does not reciprocate, a courageous conversation will be required. You will also need patience. I have lived in cultures where people see marriage as outdated. I have lived in cultures where people believe that no matter what happens, you must stay married. My parents were divorced when I was seven, and I am so happy they are with people now who make them happy!

I have explored and lived on both sides of this relationship paradigm. I believe marriage is the most important miracle of my life. I believe we are meant to share the journey with someone in the most intimate way. Safety is found in this beauty. We all want to feel safe. Start writing down five things you are grateful for about the people you are sharing your life with.

Are you in a relationship that's important to you, but you're having a hard time communicating? Communication is the cause of most relationship turmoil. As a financial advisor for 18 years, I would often be in the middle of marital debates about money, but the real core issue had nothing to do with money. People are running so hard and fast right now that they forget to talk to each other inside their own homes. Money is an easy way to manifest this truth. On average, a human makes about 22 buying decisions a day. This could be what kind of coffee to buy in the morning, whether to get new curtains, you name it. A lot of married couples communicate more often about these buying decisions than they do about the core issues in life.

Let's have fun with this one. Have you ever gotten in a fight with your spouse about the smallest thing in the world, like what color curtains to buy, but the fight has nothing to do with what you're arguing about? And then it spirals into all these weird things as you keep stacking a case against each other? I use this as a reference because this happened to Shannon and me one time. The surface issue was that I needed blackout curtains because there were so many lights in our neighborhood that it was affecting the quality of my sleep. The core issue was I needed help. I did not care about the curtains. Shannon had all of these specific desires around the curtains, and I had a need, which was that I didn't want the light to come in. It escalated because Shannon cared about what the curtains looked like, while I did not feel heard because I wanted to sleep better.

Communication is very hard when you're living with someone full-time. You take for granted certain parts of that experience because you live together. We assume the other person should know what we're going through. Well, it's impossible to read people's minds. We've all tried to help someone with a problem, but when we find our perceived solution, the person looks at us and says, "That wasn't even the problem," or "I don't know what you're doing over there."

Shannon and I are so passionate about talking to one another. We have three kids. They are all very intense. Shannon and I are very intense. We own a company together. We do everything as a family. We stayed in an RV, which was 410 square feet, and we traveled all around the country in the middle of COVID-19. Small spaces require communication. Everything and every part of the day has to have utility because you're living in such tight quarters. Shannon and I have conflicts. Every marriage has conflict. Every relationship has conflict.

If the relationship is worth having and you are in conflict, the first thing I want you to do is tell the person the things about them you are grateful for or write them down. The ease of this will depend on your relationship with the person. Write down, *"I am grateful for you,"* and leave it as a note. If you're married and in conflict, every morning, leave a note on their pillow telling them the five things about them you are grateful for. If you do that for 20 days in a row, whatever conflict you're currently in will be closer to a resolution.

Shannon and I do this verbally. We'll go on a walk and hold hands, and we'll start telling each other the things that we are grateful for. The more conflict that we're in, the funnier this exercise is. It is a very funny experience to be mad at someone and then tell them the things that you are grateful for about them. After about 20 minutes, we're good. We kiss and make up because the thing that was causing the turmoil almost always has nothing to do with us.

Is an external force creating tension in your relationships? Close relationships are our safe place. Raising children can set off countless triggers. A good example of this is our children going to school. As parents, we can hear from the teacher that our children are very well-behaved. Then, they come home and release all of the built-up tension. They feel safe to have every emotion they were holding back all day long. In this moment, you have to realize you're doing a good job because the person in your life who's having that tantrum with you feels safe with you. Now, you will have to create boundaries if this person is consuming too much or taking too much from you in this safety. You will have to tell them it is too much, and that's where therapists, third parties, and coaches help people hold space because you might be going through massive shifts.

In a relationship with someone, whether a client, my wife, my friend, or my children, if there is conflict, turn towards the hard. I am a loving and kind human. Addressing conflict is the last thing I want to do in my day. However, every time there is a ripple or an undercurrent of frustration in a relationship, I run into that head first and address it. This behavior helps the relationship grow and strengthen. Almost every time there's tension, it's because of a communication breakdown.

The number one tool I use to explore conflict resolution is asking questions. When I'm experiencing relationship tension, if I try to solve the problem through statements, the tension usually spirals up. If you are in a situation where your anxiety is increasing because of the tension you are having with someone, ask them questions. Ask them, "What is your number one trigger right now?" Then be quiet! The person will tell you everything you need to know to determine whether you are the solution to their problem. And if you are, you can either choose to engage in this moment and start working on the solution, or you could say, "Thank you for making me aware of this situation. I currently do not have the solution. Can I think about this? Then I will get back to you on how I think I can help."

Separating from the problem temporarily will provide a fast track to the solution. However, if your intuition tells you at that moment, "I got this," then go ahead and solve the problem, bury it, make it go away through communication, and then move on.

The most important step in this process is not to get a third party involved if you can handle it. Triangular conversations waste the most time in your day. If someone is creating conflict in your life and you ask six people what you should do about it, they're going to give you six different answers. Have the courage to call the person who's causing the problem or have a cup of coffee or lunch with them. Head straight into that conflict, and I promise it will be a shortcut.

Now, there's one small caveat to this. There may be times in life when you need support, and I'm not saying that's a bad thing. Some events require counsel. So, embrace that. The conflict I'm talking about consists of microaggressions, the small problems that people spend so much time in their daily lives talking about instead of addressing. Those are the ones where you could probably take out a couple of hours of your day of inefficiency and double down on communication.

Communication and gratitude have been the fastest shortcuts for me to grow love and kindness in every relationship in my life. In the end, when we drive love and kindness into our relationships, we all see the beauty in human resolve. We are all seeking pleasure and avoiding pain. That looks different for all of us, but the idea can help us communicate better. Seeking to understand other peoples' pain and pleasure will build lasting relationships.

CHAPTER 5

The End of Our Personal Paradox

In April of 2019, we moved four miles from our neighborhood. Shannon and I were looking to live more in nature, and this required finding some land. We did not think it would be right down the road. We visited the house, and I remember tearing up in the driveway as I stared into the woods. It was the same feeling I got that day when I visited my college, SJU. I knew this was where we should live and take in nature.

We left, and by that afternoon, we had a list of things we needed to do to sell the house: get a new doorknob, paint the wall, fix the toilet in the basement we never use. You know, all the stuff we do for others to sell our house that we were unwilling to do for ourselves. It's a strange truth I still have not figured out.

That weekend, I was in GO mode. We completed our list over the next seven days. Shannon has her real estate license, so she was able to coordinate photos and get the house on the market eight days after I had stood in the driveway of the new house. Our house sold the next day, and we put in an offer on the house in the woods the day after that. When things fall into place like this, you have to do it. It was like the entire path had been laid out before us, and all we had to do was take the first step.

During all of this, Shannon was pregnant with our third little one. Needless to say, people thought we were a little crazy. Little did they know, but these external steps had been in motion for 18 months. It looked fast to our family and friends, but it was at the exact right time for us.

We moved in May, and our son Grayson was born June 3. Perfect timing! There were so many questions from people around us. We now lived down a dirt road on a 14-acre lot that was in a land trust to preserve it. People would ask, "What about your kids growing up in a neighborhood? Does your car get dirty on a dirt road?" Of course! "Did you think about the school district? Did you know you cannot modify your land in a land trust?" From the outside looking in, perhaps what we had done looked irrational. From the inside looking out, those questions looked irrational.

I think this was such a shift for others because they saw our family "brand" get turned upside down in a couple of months. We stopped living out that paradox and started living out our truth. You can imagine how strange this was for us, too. There were times when we got defensive and felt the need to justify our choices. At times, this was frustrating, but we were so confident in our truth that the answers came naturally. There was no strategy with the explanation. This was one of the first times in my life where I was not thinking about what other people thought of me when I shared who I was. Once I felt this, there was no turning back.

With these massive personal shifts complete, it was time to turn my attention to my professional life. More to come. In the meantime, I started being home more. I stopped working nights and made my children a priority. I still left early in the morning, but Shannon needed me home at dinnertime. We had a newborn, an almost two-year-old, and a four-year-old.

I loved being home, and we found great joy in being outside. Our kids refused to wear clothes, as all little ones do, but now we were down a dirt road. It was not easy for me to transition into this more intense role as a Dad. I was used to seeing the kids two nights a week and on weekends. The more I saw them, the more I wanted to be seen. This began a professional awakening that would play out in the coming months.

For the first time in my adult life, I felt safe at home and a hundred percent myself. My home and family became my top priorities. You would have thought this would have been true after the birth of our four-year-old, Madelyn, but I still needed to grow up quite a bit. Our home became our place of peace, and I stopped justifying it. We knew exactly what it meant to us, and now we did not have to prove it. Our home became our family sanctuary.

I am beyond grateful for the process we experienced in May of 2019. It prepared us for the massive shift that was coming in March of 2020. The world was about to change drastically. I remember watching the news, thinking, *Is this real life?* At the beginning of COVID, I was scared. The information was so fragmented that the only thing we knew to do was cocoon ourselves on our little dirt road. We did this for 45 days. In May, we decided that this did not feel consistent with what people in other parts of the US were experiencing. We were hearing that the Northeast was handling lockdowns and guidelines differently than the West.

Being the seekers that we are, we decided to rent a house in Phoenix, AZ, for a month and go find out for ourselves. We wanted to see how different cultures were reacting to this very sad time in human history. We weighed the risks as a young family and chose to go. This was the beginning of every "norm" being flipped on its head in our family. We returned to Pennsylvania in June, and it felt more extreme because of what we had just seen in Arizona. It felt like we were in two different worlds.

On July 9, 2020, on my 34th birthday, we bought our first RV (Winnie). It was an A-class. I traded in my Range Rover Sport for a Jeep Wrangler. For the money people, the RV plus Jeep payment was the same monthly cost as the Range Rover Sport. I could get a house on wheels and circle back on my love of Jeep Wranglers for the same monthly outlay!

We left PA in August of 2020 and went to explore Montana, Idaho, and Utah. We tried going to the West Coast but got turned around in the smoke in Oregon. We were on the road for 40 days on the first trip and saw so many things with almost no one around. The day we visited Mount Rushmore, there were ten people there. We found ourselves in the middle of nowhere more often than not. We could carry a good amount of food, so isolation was always an option. This trip changed the trajectory of our entire lives.

We came back to PA in the fall and then went to Florida for the winter. Clients still wanted to do video calls. I believe it is easier to parent in motion. Since I could be on video calls anywhere, we stayed in motion. My office changed almost every week. We were meeting amazing, like-minded families, and the world started to make sense to us again.

In July of 2021, we decided to sell the RV. My father-in-law and I drove to FL from PA to sell Winnie because I'd gotten a good price. It was the last adventure with Winnie, and I thought we were closing that chapter. We put our kids into traditional school and started a home renovation. We recommitted to living in the place we were from. This lasted four months. As we fell back into this rhythm, we began "going through the motions." We have all had this feeling. The company we were building, The Motion of Gratitude, is the opposite of this feeling. We could not stay in this mindset, selling something we were not living out ourselves.

In November 2021, I was at the home of a client who is also a very good friend. She happens to own an RV, too. She looked into my eyes and said, "You are the unhappiest I have seen you." This hit me hard. The truth is required, and it hurts. She looked deep into my soul and said, "You guys need to get back out on the road."

In an instant, I felt total alignment. She was right. Why had we assumed we could put all this knowledge back in a box and put it on the shelf? I called Shannon while driving home, and with all the passion and conviction in the world, I said, "We need to get back out on the road."

There was a 10-second pause, and then Shannon replied, "I am in!"

With that, we started planning. The following week, I saw that a black GMC 3500 had been traded in at the local dealership over the Thanksgiving holiday. This was a very hard truck to find at the time. I told Shannon I would stop in after dropping Madelyn off at school. Madelyn said, "Dad, can you drop me off at school in the Jeep today? I want one last ride." I guess we have trained our kids to expect change.

Six days after sitting in my client's home, we owned a truck. Now, we needed the RV. We decided to get a fifth wheel because we wanted more space. Winnie was "go fast, see a lot." The new rig, which we call HQ (the mobile headquarters for The Motion of Gratitude), was about "go slow, stay longer." We found the one we wanted, and it happened to only be three hours from the house. Shannon and I drove there the first week of December. They had the Grand Design model we wanted, so we said yes and set up delivery to pick the rig up in two weeks.

We decided we would go to the Florida Keys for Christmas. You can imagine we had our family members' heads spinning. We are beyond grateful for our family's support. Do not get me wrong; there has been resistance, but there has also been an incredible respect for the choices we've made.

Just as I had never driven a 40-foot boat, I had never pulled a 43-foot RV down the road. These YESES required me to learn a lot of information in a very short amount of time. Safety and preparation are the only ways I can do these things. I must understand so I can thrive.

Off to Florida, we went! We had the most relaxing Christmas, and we were with our people. I love hanging out with nomads. It has been the most aligned tribe I have been a part of. The kids were still enrolled in school at this point. Driving north 12 days later, we had to make a choice. Live in the newly renovated house, keep our kids in school, and go back to traditional living OR go back on the road.

After getting the house and the RV ready, we left on a freezing day, January 23, 2022. We set no return date. Here we go again! We spent the winter in Florida and then worked our way across the South to Texas.

After 50 days in the RV, we were feeling some cabin fever. We'd felt a pull to move to Utah in 2021, but it had not worked out. The pull had started again, but it was more intense this time. Shannon was researching the state, and I was open to the move. In April of 2022, we decided that if we did not do it now, we never would. When we got to Utah, it was still cold, and we rented houses and breathed in the culture.

The home renovation was completed while we were on the road. Shannon had designed her dream kitchen, and now it had been built. We cooked in that kitchen one time, the night before we moved. Shannon stayed in Utah with the two little ones while Madelyn and I flew to PA and got the house ready to sell. There were so many moving parts!

Our house sold in a week, but we had not found a house in Utah yet. For 24 hours, we were "homeless." Then Shannon found the home we own now. In the middle we had to live in a rental for 30 days. The amount of things that had to go right for this to happen makes me laugh out loud. I do not want to mislead you. We were not wealthy during this process. We were traveling and building a company the whole time. We needed a lot of divine intervention to make this our reality! We moved into our house in Utah the night before Grayson's third birthday. I could not believe it had only been three years since we had moved into the house down the dirt road, three weeks before he was born.

I will share what's happened to us since so you can see how this adventure has unfolded. Although our house is in Utah, we still do not like the cold. If you have not been to Utah in the spring, summer, or fall, you have to check it out. Utah is an adult playground. There is adventure around every corner. It is also an incredible place for families!

On December 8, 2022, we loaded up the RV to head to the East Coast for winter. We spent 95 days on the road, our longest trip. I went to Costa Rica in February of 2023 while my family stayed in the RV in Florida. The second part of this book will be all about that trip. It is now winter of 2024, and I am finishing this book at a home we rented in Costa Rica for five months..

I feel like I have lived multiple lives since March 2020. COVID was a catalyst for change for our family that I never saw coming. Through all of the ordeal, our family learned to be present in every moment. Living in Gratosis and feeling perspective in motion. When we are all in motion, we thrive. Perhaps my wife and I have created adrenaline junkies in our kids, but they are going to keep us young, and they are happy!

Are you "going through the motions"? Has creative energy left your daily mindset? We have all been there! If you are looking to make a change because something does not "feel right," here are the steps to take:

1. Write down everything you are grateful for about your situation.
2. Write down all the things that had to GO RIGHT for you to be where you are today.
3. Identify what your definition of Gratosis is.
    a. Gratosis: process, state, or condition of gratitude
4. Reconnect to your definition of Gratosis.
    a. My example: Gratosis = Sovereignty.

   b. When I feel the freedom to operate, I feel ALIVE!
5. Write down all the ways you can step back into your power and your Gratosis mindset.
6. Surround yourself with people cheering FOR you.
7. Once the creativity starts coming back into your awareness, you are DOING IT!

Addressing the personal paradox is the gateway to understanding if there's anything to do regarding the professional paradox. I've always first grown personally, then professionally, and finally financially. I have discovered that if you get that out of order, the process does not work.

Over my 18 years of coaching, many of my clients first want to grow financially and then personally. Or they want to first grow financially, then professionally, and then personally. Everyone who gets this out of order has to go the long way.

I ended my personal paradox by doing the personal work first. Shannon and I had made so many pivots. We had lived on the main line of Philadelphia, which was one of my dreams growing up. Then we bought "the big house." We did not live in 50% of that house. Then we moved down the dirt road and lived in the woods. That was really the big pivot. Shannon and I are both introverts. We like privacy, and we love to control our energy. We loved to walk out our front door into the same energy that was inside our house. This isn't for everyone, but it was for us.

Then COVID happened, ending every personal paradox. We did not choose to make this change. Buying an RV was one of our greatest teaching moments. We traveled all over the United States, seeing 36 states, and understanding every culture and how it was dealing with lockdowns. We saw that everyone creates their own worldview. We could have become recluses down that dirt road in the woods. We had our little energy bubble, but our intuitions told us, "GO LIVE."

Perhaps you, too, find yourself going through the motions, waking up each day and not knowing what you're doing or why. You might be hitting the snooze button every morning. You might be going to the same coffee shop, and you don't like their coffee. You might be surfing the internet without even knowing why. You might be eating food that you know is not good for you, but it's convenient, so you eat it anyway. I have done all of these things.

The major pivot for me was the understanding that life has to be more than this. Some people call that a midlife crisis. I call it a one-third-life wake up because my goal is to live to be a hundred. I knew that life had to be more. I refused to keep chasing a unicorn up a mountain. I had gotten to the top of my first mountain, and there was no unicorn. Instead, there was a bigger mountain on the other side.

For me, that mountain was fatherhood. No matter how much money I made, the only things the kids cared about were: Am I present? Do I love them? Am I having fun? And do they get to eat, sleep, and go to the bathroom? This simplified my life in such a beautiful way. That does not mean I could wrap my head around it.

If you find yourself going through the motions, you have to do the exercise we've already talked about.

Step one: get out a pen and a piece of paper and write down everything in your life that is going right for you.

Now, some people might say, "I have nothing." I promise you, there's something. For one thing, you're alive. You're breathing. There have been moments in my life where the first thing I wrote in my gratitude journal was, *"I am grateful to be alive today,"* because I could not think of anything else. They were dark times, but they are part of the reality of this walk.

If you write down five things you're grateful for every day for 28 days, you will kick yourself out of this mindset. Your brain will have to get creative. If you really want to take it to a hard place, never write down the same thing for 28 days. This is the beginning of the process for you to get yourself out of going through the motions. The reason our company is called The Motion of Gratitude is that it's the opposite of going through the motions of life.

Step two: identify your definition of Gratosis. Gratosis, a word we made up, means the process, state, or condition of gratitude. Science has proven your prefrontal cortex is glowing differently when you're living in a state of gratitude, bliss, and joy. You might have experienced this when your children were born, when you bought something you really wanted, when you moved into your first house, or when you got accepted to college. A physical reaction caused by a mental state, goosebumps, happy tears, laughter, when you might have to sit down because the moment doesn't feel real—that is Gratosis.

The definition of Gratosis, for me, has changed. My boat's name was *Gratosis*. I no longer own it. My current definition of Gratosis is sovereignty, the ultimate freedom for me and my family to live out a life of happiness, abundance, and love. That's me.

Where you are in your life right now will determine what Gratosis means to you. I have discovered that for older people, particularly people in their 70s, 80s, and 90s, Gratosis usually revolves around people, relationships, and being with others. It doesn't matter what your definition of Gratosis is. Gratosis is the feeling, the state of consciousness that makes you tick. It is the reason you get up in the morning. You're either chasing Gratosis or you are in it. Both are very valid pursuits. The ultimate goal is to live in Gratosis, and that takes work.

Step three: stay connected to Gratosis. The only way I've been able to stay connected to my Gratosis, my sovereignty, is to acknowledge it daily, multiple times.

The word "sovereignty" is everything to me. It's all I think about. Every time I make a choice, I ask myself, is this creating freedom in my life or for my future self? If the answer is no, I don't do it. The power of the no will create the beauty of all the yeses you pursue.

Step four: at the end of the day, write down and acknowledge every moment that you were living in Gratosis. An end-of-the-day gratitude practice will start to really unlock the key to your psyche. Start your day with gratitude and end your day with gratitude. Writing down all the things you're grateful for will align your definition of Gratosis with your state of being. Bookending your day with the beauty of this state of consciousness will lock in all the positive benefits.

In addition, it is key to keep all screens out of your bedroom. TVs inside our bedrooms are a major disruptor to everything that I'm sharing with you. If you turn the TV on every night after you lie in bed, you are not giving your brain the opportunity to wind down, and you're not setting an intention for your sleep pattern. By gratitude journaling at the end of your day, you're setting an intention for your subconscious dream state. You're going into the dream state from a state of gratitude. Again, it is not possible for you to be grateful and depressed at the same time. The intentionality around this practice will be life-changing.

Step five: surround yourself with people who are cheering for you. As you're coming back into this power, you're going to find that there's a lot of disruption in your life, personally, professionally, and financially. The personal paradox is the hardest one to unwind. You need a support system of people who are cheering for you. Find your tribe. Find the people who are doing this type of work and be with them.

Humans are pack animals. We require a community to thrive. Isolation is the core of most disruption and sadness in our lives. When you're going through massive pivots, if you choose to isolate yourself, you're in trouble.

Being around people doesn't mean you have to talk to them. For example, if you're going through a massive personal shift that involves health, join clubs. If you're a runner, join a running club. If you're a biker, find a biking club.

I can bike 25 miles and not say a word to another human. We find joy in being together and doing our inner work side by side. We'll stop in the middle, drink water, and have a snack. It's all good. We're doing it together. And then sometimes, I'll get on my bike and ride with people, and we'll talk the whole time about serious life issues: raising kids, growing our businesses, you name it. Community is so critical to these massive life pivots.

Step six: be creative. Creativity is the number one sign of success. When you get back into the creative flow of life, you are moving in the right direction. When you feel your creative force coming back, celebrate this new version of you! You might start listening to music more often. You might start drawing. You might start getting creative with your hands and building something. These are all key indicators that you're coming back into your power.

We humans love to be creative. The arts are part of the beauty of life. In our modern times, we have found ourselves in a position where we are very linear in our thinking. We wake up at the same time every morning. We go to work to do the same job every day. We eat the same food. Everything is the same. This is the opposite of creative force.

We need both a routine and a creative force. The scale needs to be tipped back to the center. When you feel yourself able to meditate, pray, journal, write, or color, you are coming back to LIFE. These actions are clear signs that your brain is activated differently, and you're coming into a solution, which is an upgrade of your current self at the current age.

Be playful. Watch children. Watch how curious they are. Look at their eyes. Seek eye contact. Children are your teachers. Whether they are yours, a niece or a nephew, or a friend's child, it doesn't matter. When I watch my children play, and I see how curious and innocent they are, I remember that's how I'm supposed to be. Children are my greatest teachers, and I promise that they can be yours, too.

CHAPTER 6

The Professional Paradox Ends

I was stuck in a professional paradox: I felt safe at home, but I pretended to be someone else at work. I worked hard to change the culture of my team. Changing the culture from the top down is easy. Changing culture from the bottom up, not so much. This caused a struggle within that had to be solved. Once I solved it at home, it became clear I had to do the same at work. The details about work are not important, but the outcome is. I had to get rid of this struggle, but I knew this would be one of the hardest choices in my life.

I started in the financial services industry when I was 20. I am beyond blessed to say I have been in this industry for 18 years. I am incredibly grateful for the company that taught me the ropes, and I would not be where I am today without them. I would also not have the business I was able to monetize at 33 if it were not for my time and education. So much good came from my time there. I would say my exit was like buying the house: I just had to take the first step.

There is a part of me that I have not totally figured out yet. I am influenced heavily by the culture I am in. I know most of them are, but my friends can often see through the cultural forest while I cannot. I was in a sales culture and managed salespeople. It was a culture focused on winning, which is why I was able to get where I was at a young age.

There came a point, though, when I'd had enough. Measuring outcomes through client ROIs or my teams' sales had gotten very old. All I wanted to do was teach my clients to find their truth. If that involved me being their financial planner, great. In addition, as a manager, if my advisors were not hitting their sales numbers, perhaps they were dealing with a personal issue, or maybe this was not the right career for them. It was that simple to me. I spent more time coaching people out of the business than into it.

When people are happy and doing what they believe they are designed to do, they succeed. If not, they need to recalibrate and change. I was spending more time defending my coaching style than I was coaching. I was spending more time strategizing than I was implementing. The whole thing made me want to go home to my safe place to enjoy my time with my family. The challenge before me was that I had to thrive financially for us to live the life we enjoyed, but I also had to enjoy my work life, so I stayed engaged. The environment had become toxic enough that I had to at least look elsewhere.

I took the first step, and again, the path was laid out before me. One call led to another, which led to one interview, then another, and then a third. We were on a staycation, watching my mom's house and the horses. I was on the phone and doing interviews. Shannon and I had a ton of time to reflect and talk through the situation.

I had to decide: should I go to another company with a similar approach as my current one, go independent, or become an employee advisor? For years, I had been taught that employee advisors lose control of their destiny, so I was the most skeptical about this last idea. On the plus side, there would be a liquidation event that would create the start-up capital for our other company, which we had been working on for two years. The downside was that I could not bring my staff.

I knew I did not want to open door number one because it would only result in a lot of the same. If I opened door number two, it would require the most work with a young family. Door number three felt like the best choice. The culture was right. The client's focus was aligned with my interests at the time. I would be able to level up in a big way financially, and Shannon and I would get to fund a project that would be a major part of our life journey.

After endless internal debate and sleepless nights, I chose door number three. I was scared! I tried to stop myself at least a hundred times in my head—and several times out of my head. Shannon had to do a lot of listening as I relentlessly gamed out all the possible outcomes. Without her support, this change would never have happened.

Letting my employees go worked out. I would never have hired them without believing they were talented. I knew they would end up in great spots. We still communicate on a regular basis, and our relationships have stayed intact. This was by far one of my biggest challenges, and I am very grateful they do not hold it against me.

Next, I had to resign. The company was not used to such resignations, and I doubt they expected mine. From the outside looking in, they knew I had been facing challenges, but I do not believe they thought it would get to this point. This was my first legal experience, where lawyers taught me what to say, what not to, and how to leave. This was very unnatural for me. I thought I could just walk away and people would be happy for me. I was self-employed, after all. I am grateful for those attorneys, and after a couple of weeks of awkwardness, the process played out fine.

I resigned at 7:30 in the morning, and then I was able to announce to all my clients that I was leaving. I could not ask them for their business after years of helping them. The 30 days that followed tested me at every level. As an adult, crying was a very rare occurrence. However, I cried quite a bit during those 30 days, and very few of those tears were tears of joy.

A professional change was required to keep up with all the personal changes. I thought I would be at the company I had moved to for ten years. After all, I had signed a 10-year contract. When you read about what I went through in part two of this book, you will better understand why I had to get out of that 10-year contract.

This was my first time working for a publicly traded company, and it simply did not align with my thinking. I understand bottom-line thinking and expense management. It is required to meet the expectations of the shareholders. In the end, I cared more about my clients than the shareholders. I have never measured a client's worth by the money on their balance sheet. I measure their IRR in my life by the joy we experienced working towards the united goal of financial freedom as THEY have defined it. After three years and 10 months in the corporate financial channel, I went independent. I will share that story so you can experience the synchronicities and divine comedy that played out.

I realized I was not living out my definition: Gratosis = Sovereignty. A sales culture drove my environment when I was in the agency channel. In the employee channel, the bottom-line thinking was to do what was best for the shareholders. I was losing my sovereignty because of the employee bureaucracy and bottom-line thinking. This led me to face a fear I'd had in 2019: I knew being an independent financial planner was the only way to truly operate as a fiduciary at every level, but I simply did not have the confidence to do it when I made my first change.

I met my current partner, joining his firm in 2023, through a string of serendipitous events that still blow my mind every time I reflect on them. I am so grateful to have met this man and the team he has put around him. His courage to stand up for what he believes in has allowed me to find a home for my clients. I know the team cares for them the way I care for them. He created a bridge for me to step fully into my role in The Motion of Gratitude while fulfilling the promises I had made to clients over 18 years. Many financial planners who move into new roles have to walk away from their clients. This firm has allowed me to walk beside them while knowing their financial needs are taken care of in every way.

My daily focus has not shifted to The Motion of Gratitude. I have mentored and coached people since my second job as assistant manager at a sporting goods store when I was 15. I have always enjoyed responsibility and thrived in it. When I did financial planning, people would tell me their life stories, but I would be constrained to helping them with their money. The Motion of Gratitude allows me to help people "Feel the Impact" of having an intentional gratitude practice and living in their definition of Gratosis.

I believe one of the biggest threats to humanity as we move into the world of artificial intelligence is BOREDOM. When humans are bored, we tend to do very strange things, and a lot of them revolve around vices. I believe AI will create more free time for people, and we will have to learn to manage our minds in the quiet and find joy in the little things again.

I also believe people will have to start pulling AWAY from social media in the quest. This means we will need to fill our time in different ways. The lost art of gardening, reading, and building things with your hands will become relevant again.

This transition to an older cycle will require an understanding of your mind in a way that you might not have fully explored YET. In this process, people are going to be looking for guides to help them. I pray I am honored to be a helpful part of this transition. I want to help people return to the center of their lives and smile more. Life is hard, and sad things happen. We only control our reactions. Gratosis is the mindset where you know the flat tire you got is helping you miss out on something that you were NOT supposed to be going to. Gratosis is doing random acts of kindness from your heart to see the smile on a stranger's face.

Are you currently in a career where you find yourself going through the motions? Have you stopped taking care of your mind and body in pursuit of financial reward? I did. I chased the money unicorn up the mountain. There was no unicorn, only a bigger mountain on the other side. The mountain I choose to climb now revolves around being a husband and father, eating good food, moving my body, meditating, praying, and expressing gratitude. If we play the human game full time, the money game will work out! This requires trust, and there are days when fear creeps in for me, too.

If you find yourself going through the motions in your professional life, do the following:

1. Write down everything you are grateful for in your professional situation.
2. Write down all the things that had to GO RIGHT for you to be where you are today.
3. Identify what your definition of Gratosis is.
4. Reconnect with your definition of Gratosis.
5. Write down all the ways you can step back into your power and your Gratosis mindset.
6. Surround yourself with people cheering FOR you.
7. Once creativity returns to your awareness, you are DOING IT!

NOTE: An important note on the personal and professional shifts.

1. Work the personal shift first. Get centered personally BEFORE you make any professional shifts.
2. In the beginning, your definition of personal Gratosis may look different from your professional one.
    a. Transitioning towards alignment is a process.
3. Be GENTLE with yourself. This will take time and energy. Some days, you will feel uncertain. The more uncomfortable you are, the more you know you are DOING IT!

4. The crumbling – things that you thought defined you will fall away. As you come into the updated version of yourself, you will face old parts of yourself. Thank those versions of you, and do not attach. Every choice you made was part of the process to get you to this moment.
    a. Example: I used alcohol as a tool to suppress my real feelings. It worked. It helped me through chapters of my life. In my current life phase, alcohol does not serve me. I choose not to drink it, but I do not get mad at myself for using it in the past.
5. People will NOT understand what you are doing. The more you share, the harder it will be. Find a coach with whom you can share what you are going through. Every time I have made a major life shift, the first thing I do is find a person I respect who has already done what I want to do, and I ask them for help!

If you have gone through the personal evolution into your higher state of consciousness, this step is going to be easy, and it is the natural progression.

I was a financial planner for 18 years. I loved it in the beginning. I had so much passion for helping people find financial freedom as they defined it. It was all about serving people. I loved being in people's homes. I loved meeting their kids, playing with their dogs, and sitting at their kitchen table. I loved going to businesses, touring factories, walking with the owners, looking them in the eye, seeing the people who worked there, and being a part of the community. These things inspired me to grow my business and help my clients grow theirs. That changed abruptly in March 2020 when I found myself living inside of a computer.

This change was not for me. It changed everything about being a financial planner. I missed driving around in my car, running from meeting to meeting, seeing businesses, being in boardrooms. I missed every part. I did not choose to change my business model. The change was forced upon me. I felt like I was living inside a computer screen every day.

There was a duality in this truth. I had more free time to think about what I wanted. I also realized that adventure fuels my soul. My work was creating adventure. Now, my personal life needed to be the source of that reality. I said to Shannon, "I can't do this. If we're going to be going through the motions of my professional life, we need to get out and see the world."

We transformed a very hard time into a positive outlook and bought an RV. All I needed was Wi-Fi. If I was going to be stuck in a computer box every day, staring at other people in their computer boxes, at least I could be in motion and see new environments, new states, the mountains, the beaches, the beauty of America.

That was how I was able to stay in the game for four years during the COVID-19 cultural change. Making that choice was the catalyst for me making a professional change. I was growing and evolving. For years, I had helped people with their money. Now that I was out LIVING, people were asking me all kinds of different questions. I was having more fun sharing my life story, and talking about money became an obligation rather than a passion.

All of my conversations with clients revolved around their dreams and passions, and then everything would come back to money because that was my job. I woke up every morning and said, "I'm so tired of talking about money." My two triggers, as I discovered, are fear and money, yet I was managing other people's fears around money for a living. I was stuck in a loop that I could not pull out of.

And then 2022 happened. The stock market was down. It didn't make sense to me. I had moved a lot of money into assets based on other people's guidance. I am a highly emotional human, and I could no longer take what my clients were going through on a daily basis and carry that for them. We all come to these moments in life where we have to make a choice. We can choose to keep doing what we've done – in my case, for 18 years because I needed to provide financially for my family – or we can make a change.

I had built a business with passive revenue. I had earned all my designations: CFP, CLU, CHFC, and CASL. I had done the work to become an expert in my field. But it was no longer making me happy. I was going through the motions, and I resented what I was doing on a daily basis. I found myself avoiding the required tasks to be a successful financial planner. I found myself hating checking my email. Some days, I could not open my laptop.

I was so grateful for my assistant because she protected me as I went through this evolution. She would filter my emails and text me. Relationships are so important as you go through these trials. Without her help, the wheels would have come off the bus.

If you find yourself in a similar situation, there are several steps you can take to get through it:

1. Do exactly what you did at the end of your personal paradox. Write down everything you're grateful for about your professional situation. Live in gratitude. I am so grateful for my 18 years as a financial planner. It taught me everything that I needed to know to be right here, right now. And it's also preparing me for what's next.
2. Write down everything that's going right in your life today because of what you've done.
3. Identify your definition of Gratosis if you haven't already done so.
4. Stay connected to your definition of Gratosis. Continue writing down every day what you're grateful for and surround yourself with the right people.
5. Make sure that you are focusing on the creative solution for where you will go next professionally. The answers will come once you're locked into the creative forces.

If you're coming at this from a place of fear and scarcity, you cannot find your next step. Whether you believe this is happening to you or for you, you need a process. Reframe the situation in your brain to say, *No matter what's happening right now, it's for me, for who I am to become next.*

Now, there are some additional steps with the professional shift. First, you have to make a personal shift. What does that look like? Finding your definition of Gratosis; taking care of your mind, body, and soul; meditation; gratitude; prayer; eating the right food; getting outside every day; breathing into mother nature; absorbing sunshine; getting your vitamin D; drinking enough water—these are all personal requirements for you to be totally aligned with the decision-making process you're going to have to engage in to make this professional shift. Intention is the most important part of this process. Then, understand your definition of Gratosis.

Gratosis = Sovereignty for me. My professional shift required freedom to live the life I wanted and embrace the values that aligned with my soul. I immediately rejected any construct that took away that power as a premise for moving forward, no matter how much money it meant giving up.

I hear this all the time: "It must be easy for you because you've made money, and now you're speaking from that side of the equation." I have lived both sides of the coin. I've built a business without any money. Then I made money. Then I spent it all to build a business, and now I'm doing it again without a lot of money. I'm living out the same cycle. I have more confidence now, though, because of my life experience. Frankly, this time, it has been so much harder than before because, when I did it the first time, I was not married and did not have any children. The choices Shannon and I are making today are very intentional, and the responsibility to make sure we do not blow up our lives is so much more intense than when I was 21 years old.

There's an important thing to know about this shift. There will be crumbling. You are falling away from your old self and designing a new one.

All of us will go through this crumbling process as we go through our reinvention. Such crumbling is required to build. Clear the land and build the foundation.

I worked very hard to build the life I had. But when I realized it was not the life I wanted to live anymore, I walked away with a smile. That does not mean there was no sacrifice. People who thought you were one version of yourself and then see a different version will not understand it. They will think you're crazy. Sometimes, I think I'm crazy too.

Whenever I feel that way, I pick up the phone and call a person who has done what I'm doing. Usually, it's a 10-minute phone conversation, and it resets my line of thinking, getting me back on track. Or I will talk to Shannon because she and I are building this business together, and she feels crazy sometimes. Communication is critical for this phase of your evolution.

Money will become funky in this phase. If you continue to play the money game all day long, you will lose. As a financial planner for 18 years, I watched this every single day. The people who attach to their money always wake up one day and feel like it is a giant trap.

Unfortunately, that happens to most people the day they retire. They've spent 35, 45, 50 years of their life accumulating money and building a nest egg. I can't tell you how many times someone retired and, within the year, got sick, had cancer, went through a traumatic event with a child or a grandchild, and everything that they thought they were working for was turned on its head in a minute.

I promise you that their balance sheet could not solve these problems. It can help. If you're going through massive life pivots and you have a balance sheet, it will make it easier. But there's a reason why people who have a lot of money spend it all and go broke. It's because they haven't done the personal work. They've played the money game, and there are no rules, and everyone loses because we don't take money with us.

So, as you're going through the professional paradox pivot, the only thing that matters is the human game. Being a strong, vibrant human; being able to manage your nervous system; eating the correct food; knowing how important Mother Nature is to our frequency—these things are critical, and for everyone I have helped, coached, or been a part of their lives who is crushing the human game, the money always works out. So, stay centered and focused on that reality.

Another thing that might have to change is the tools in your toolbox, the tools you are using to manage your nervous system. I have been vulnerable and shared with you that alcohol was a very intentional tool for me. I am a highly emotional human, and every time I could not manage my stress or my nervous system, red wine could! The next part of this book will teach you what I had to do to break that cycle. This tool lowered my vibration, while my kids required me to operate at high vibration.

Certain tools suppress emotions. The more we push them down, the bigger the storm we create for ourselves for the future. In the next part of this book, you will learn about plant medicine, which does the opposite. It forces every single emotion that you suppress to come up and out. So, if you are using tools in your life right now that are suppressing your emotions, it's okay. Most humans are, and those tools could be social media, alcohol, recreational use of drugs, or other vices. That is more normal than not. Look at yourself in the mirror. If you can't, that's your number one goal. If you can, be gentle. Say, "I choose to be different today. I choose to stop. I choose to stop using tools that are not serving me." If you cannot do this alone, ask for help.

Our society has conditioned us to think that asking for help is a weakness. The strongest people I know are the best at asking for help. It is an honor to ask for help and to be helped. This process of changing your professional paradox is the external version of the personal paradox. It is not quiet work. When you start doing this professionally, everyone is watching. It is the external manifestation of your reality. Experiencing other people's opinions about who you are becoming is unavoidable. If you are not centered and true to yourself, you will spend more time justifying your behavior or convincing others that what you're doing is a good idea than you will be doing what you need to do.

You do not have to justify your change to anyone except for the people who love you and whom you love. Justify might not be the perfect word; you just need to explain to them what you're doing, and the people who love you will support you. They will care for you even though they might not totally get it. Your parents might not understand. Your grandparents might really not understand. That's okay. Share with them so they can be a part of your upgrade!

During the crumbling, a lot of people will get confused and fall away from your reality. And you might even find some people wanting you to fail. They are betting against you not because they want you to fail but because they are jealous that you're willing to do the work. Love those people where they're at. Pray for them daily. Acknowledge their feelings, but do not let them become the mirror that breaks you. They need to look in their own mirror and start working on their solution.

The only mirror that matters is the one that you look into in your bathroom every single morning. Look into your eyes and say, "I'm doing the very best based on this current version of myself, and I seek the solution daily."

You're growing into the best version that you've ever become. Take a deep breath, maybe shed a tear of joy, and know that you are in Gratosis.

PART 2

The Journey to Waking Up

CHAPTER 7

The River BEFORE the Waterfall

There is a RIVER *before* every WATERFALL and a RIVER *after* every WATERFALL.

- RIVER – daily practices to help us operate at high states of consciousness.
    - Examples: treating food as medicine, meditation, gratitude practice, exercise, human interaction, sleep, reducing screen time, calm breathwork, drinking enough water.
- WATERFALL – Intense moments to force clarity into our lives to leap into higher states of consciousness.
    - Examples: near-death experiences, plant medicine, intense breathwork, fasting for long periods, seminars, very intense workouts, extreme sports.

This section of the book provides a clear path into my soul. With the risk of a massive vulnerability hangover, I proceed with caution. We all go through massive shifts in life. Some of these are by accident due to an event outside of our control. Others might purposely walk into a situation knowing a massive shift is on the horizon.

For me, the beginning of this shift started in October of 2019. The peak was in February of 2023. There were so many new lessons and moments of disillusionment. The root cause was obvious, but my inability to shake the feelings was relentlessly frustrating. I would not pull up. The professional journey had become relentlessly "going through the motions." This was the first time in my life I had felt this way. My business was built on seeing people, and now I was looking at a computer screen all day. I missed going to peoples' homes and seeing their kids and pets.

We were traveling around the country in an RV. We saw so many things, and perspective in motion was in full force. With this motion came guilt. Why us? Why were we doing this and justifying our behavior to so many other people? Was it wrong? Were we hurting people by living in an RV in the middle of nowhere? We explored 36 states in a very brief period. It felt like I was in a strange social experiment that I could not get out of. We started our RV journey with a one-year-old, two-and-a-half-year-old, and almost-4-year-old. It was INTENSE, but it felt like the only right answer for our family.

Thankfully, The Motion of Gratitude was part of our lives at this juncture. Shannon created her program in July of 2018, and I was her biggest user. I would lock into my practice. It was not perfect, but it changed my life. It helped me get into great shape mentally and physically in the summer of 2019. Without her program and the work I had done with coaches, there is no way I could have shifted companies in October of 2019.

For me, The Motion of Gratitude is a river. It is a daily practice of gratitude, meditation, and a mindset to stay locked in. It works for me in the flow of life when things are making sense. The waterfall is my default setting. Waterfalls are intense, focused processes or events that force you into higher states of consciousness. The waterfall that I went OVER in February 2023 was about to rock my world in a way I never saw coming!

Note of Caution

Before I dive into my experience, I need to share some thoughts on it. I am going to share this story because it helped ME. I do not believe the modality should be used without a massive amount of research and understanding. I studied ayahuasca for almost five years. I was always intrigued by it. When I started my research, ayahuasca was not culturally accepted in the US. A few famous people shared their stories with it in 2021 and 2022, which opened my mind and heart to the idea that society was "kind of" ready for this form of healing work.

Ayahuasca has been used in Central and South America for thousands of years. It's nothing new and exciting for those cultures. Taking ayahuasca is just what you do when you need help. I spent hours listening to podcasts and watching documentaries and YouTube videos. Even with all that research, my life was about to get flipped upside down!

There are a couple of things I have learned from this healing journey. The most important is to BE GENTLE with yourself. The human brain is very sophisticated, but this blessing can be a curse as you start to explore this type of healing work. Your mind can play tricks on you, and you'll begin to question most things you thought worked a certain way. It might be to help teach a lesson or simply to understand the paradoxes of life. At many points on this journey, you will discover that, as I would say, "everything that is, the opposite is true." That statement in and of itself is confusing!

This story is not to inspire ANYONE to explore ayahuasca. I intend to encourage people to start asking themselves questions to explore the paradigms of life as a seeker. I believe knowledge leads to our truth through our intuition. The phrase "knowledge is power" has always bothered me. Knowledge can be used to enforce power. Knowledge of personal truth means that you take what you are learning to build conviction in your life choices.

Then, you use the conviction to do good. The intention behind your knowledge is EVERYTHING.

As psychedelics become more mainstream in the US, I believe we face a massive cultural risk. These plant medicines have been used for thousands of years in very sacred ceremonies. In no way do I believe recreational use of these tools should be an option for the healing journey. Without the right people to help facilitate these ceremonies, people can get lost, and their whole life can get flipped upside down.

I am so grateful for my wife because she held space for me when I returned to the US from Costa Rica. She believed in me and knew me at my core. Without her knowledge of me, my story could be very different right now. My biggest observation in the community I have gotten to know is that many people on the spiritual healing journey end up broke and single quite often. This is not the goal of these healing modalities. The goal is to end up happy in relationships, living an abundant life.

Don't get me wrong; going on this journey has led to a massive crumbling and reinvention of me personally, professionally, and financially. As I write these words, I am still in the middle of this massive shift. The irony is that I am the most centered version of myself I have ever known, AND I am still going through massive changes that require relentless patience and grace.

"What is coming is going." This is the most important phrase in my life. The more I explore WHY I see and feel the things I do, the more comes up. The more that comes up, the more I must address about myself and my relationships. It has not become a hobby to create boundaries to make people angry. It has become a requirement to be my true self. The more that comes to the surface, the more work I must do to be "clean and clear."

We have all made mistakes and hurt others, either on purpose or unintentionally. I now go into every situation saying, "This person is doing the absolute best they can do." I believe most humans inherently want the same things. We want safety and love, and all pain comes from rejection. Therefore, we chase love and kindness and avoid pain and suffering.

The last note I wanted to share is about the spiritual journey. I have relentlessly sought to understand this world. I love research. I have been blessed to travel and live in many cultures. I grew up Catholic and went to Catholic grade school, high school, and college. I have lived without faith for a while, questioning everything. I have read and researched the sacred scriptures of many religions. I have lived in Utah County with the Mormons. I spent a lot of time in Costa Rica with the divine feminine, Father Sky, and Mother Earth.

I'm sharing this because I enjoy learning about cultures and not judging their resolve to spiritual connection. I have my beliefs, and they are rooted in me. I believe every person has the right to explore their spirituality and align themselves with what feels right for them. As you read my journal notes, you will see the word "God." I believe in God. My journey in the jungle validated and strengthened that reality for ME. Please do not let that word distract you from what I believe is the value of reading my story. If it makes you feel better, replace that word with "source," "universe," or "inner voice."

My goal is to inspire people to ask questions, to challenge people to be curious, and find their inner peace. I always want to express that if you believe in everything, you believe in nothing. I seek to understand. By understanding other cultures, I respect their collective consciousness. As a consequence, I have found that people respect me. I do not believe our job is to convince one another who is right and wrong about the correct spiritual path. I believe there are many paths but very few destinations.

The foundation of my belief system is that gratitude is the gateway and destination of the spiritual journey. I believe love and kindness fuel the human experience. I believe the miracle of life is too perfect to be random, and there is a divine creator. I believe we must find harmony in the masculine and feminine, Father Sky and Mother Earth. I believe there are different religions that can help cultures on this path, and all of them started with the absolute best intentions.

In the end, I believe that my soul came from the heavens and, to the heavens, it shall return. I believe my body came from the earth and, to the earth, it shall return. While I am here, I believe my job is to spread love and kindness and be a candlelight, whether I am in a dark room or outside on a sunny day.

I share my beliefs because I believe. Faith is the opposite of fear in my world. I need my faith to say YES and keep going. I also need to surrender daily to all the unknown that can create fear in my life. I have yet to meet a human who has all the answers. Until I return to heaven, I believe my role is to seek to understand others and avoid judging their path to their center.

Let the Journey Begin

On February 18, 2023, I prepared for the unknown. I would be leaving for Costa Rica the next day to explore plant medicine. How had I gotten here? I had been researching ayahuasca for five years. It had always intrigued me, but I'd been too scared to act because of my insecurity about what other people would think. Aaron Rodgers opened this door for me. I am not a big sports fan, but I enjoy watching influential people swim against societal norms. Watching Aaron Rodgers stand in his truth somehow permitted me to stand in my own.

Here is my journal entry from that day:

"In the last 112 days, I had alcohol once. Preparing for this trip has already made me a better man. I had a couple of drinks one night when I fell back into my familiar. That was a bad choice. It made me feel terrible, and it continues

to validate my decision to live without alcohol. I have been using kava as a replacement, which helps me settle my nerves.

In the midst of parenting and traveling all around the country in an RV, I find myself reaching for some tool to calm my nervous system. This tool is still causing me to have a short fuse with the kids, so I know this is not the answer. Bio-hacking is all the rage right now. This plant is not for me. I only want to put things in my body that are natural to the earth.

Today is also day seven with no caffeine. This is much harder for me to give up than alcohol. I always used alcohol as a tool to cover up my feelings. It was very intentional all along the way. Coffee, on the other hand, fuels my morning routine. Today, I am moody and have achy joints. It is crazy to see what this plant has been masking in my reality. My body is screaming at me to change. I have been ignoring its cry for help.

I have been very open about this journey with family and friends, which leads me to believe this is the right time to embark on this journey. I do not want to hide behind a mask. Family has been very supportive while I work through 'why' I am going. In reality, I do not have the exact answer. I know I want to go back in time. I want to remember my childhood. I know life is not meant to be lived with this much anxiety and frustration. I know there is more to life than money. I know, I know, I know, but not the 'why I ended up here.' Shannon has had my back this whole time. There is almost nothing to write about regarding my reservations about my marriage. I know we go at this together.

What is coming up as I prepare?

1. *I have been more angry in the last 30 days than I can ever remember being in my life.*
2. *Why is it easier to sell life insurance than gratitude?*
3. *Am I meant to be a financial planner?*
4. *Why are we on this planet with so much evil, and why does it feel like evil is winning right now?*

5. *I'm afraid of how my body will react to the medicine.*
6. *I feel like I must have an answer for 'why' I am doing this.*

My intentions:

1. *Understand my anger. Where does it come from?*
2. *Find pure joy in being a father.*
3. *Forgive my family for any hurt I feel they have caused me.*
4. *Why do I not fear death?*
5. *Why do I believe every illness is God's way of waking up our minds through the body?*
6. *Meet fellow seekers and build a community around these friendships."*

"February 19 – Travel Day

I arrived at the retreat to find a very clean and intentional process. The place I had chosen to take this step is very well known. They combine Eastern and Western philosophy and medicine to create a 'safe' container for this type of work. People visit the retreat from all over the world.

I checked in and headed to the steam room for some thinking time. I have always loved sitting in saunas and steam rooms. Here is what came up. I will leave these thoughts at the door while I am here.

1. *Fear of money and bills.*
2. *Shannon alone with the kids.*
3. *Work and stock market.*
4. *Resistance to change.*
5. *Fear around the medicine being in my body.*

Questions coming up:

1. *Why am I here?*
2. *Are we going down the right path as a family with The Motion of Gratitude?*
3. *Why did we move across the country?*
4. *Is financial planning where my heart and energy reside?*
5. *Why am I angry?*
6. *How many generations has the masculine trauma in my family been around?"*

Have you heard the call for a deeper purpose in your life? Are you scared to answer the call? I know I was. It took me five years to book the trip to Costa Rica. I kept researching ayahuasca and watching interviews on YouTube. My whole algorithm was plant-based medicine. My Story will share that journey with you.

The call will use many different tools to help you "wake up." Is there anything calling you that would require you to step completely out of your comfort zone? If there is, and you are on the fence, I hope that this next part of the book will inspire you.

CHAPTER 8

Night 1 – Breathwork

Breathwork? I breathe all the time! Taking a class to learn to breathe seems a little silly. Someone asked me one time, "Are we going to breathe the whole time?"

My answer: "I sure hope So!"

When we lay down on our mats, we were handed a mouthpiece to keep our mouths open for 30 minutes of breathing. My first reaction: *"NO WAY. I cannot breathe like this for 30 minutes."* After the first 10 minutes, I quickly adapted and settled into an intense breathing pattern. My next thought: *What did I get myself into?!*

It was so good to cry! I had not cried in a long time. To be honest, I did not believe crying was an option for me as a man. I cried the day Shannon and I got married, when we found our house down a dirt road, and at the births of my three children. Other than that, every time I had intense emotions, I would have a beer or glass of wine.

The first experience I had in breathwork was reliving Madelyn's birth. It was like I was in a movie, watching myself as a new dad. I relived every minute of that process. I saw her hold my finger and stop crying. I saw my wife on the operating table. That was a scary day for me. It was like I had totally forgotten what happened that day. Of course, I had looked at pictures now and then, but this was different. A more mature version of myself was dropping back into my older self but with my current awareness.

The same happened with Quinn, our secondborn. I could see her eyes for the first time. I had forgotten that moment. Tears rolled down my cheeks, but I was not sobbing. It was like a river of fluid decided to flow from my eyes.

Then I got upset because I did not have the same moment for the birth of our son. This came through as a red flag. I was not fully in my body the day he was born. We had just moved into our new home, and I was "tapped out." This made me incredibly sad and would set into motion quite a bit of work to unravel this.

This process was very uncomfortable for me. My body tingled all over. I knew I could have stopped breathing so intensely, but I chose to keep going because everyone else was. Peer pressure has always been a thing for me. There are also moments where I felt like I was floating—very strange for this linear thinker. The main feelings that came up were a sense of being overwhelmed, calmness, sadness, joy, gratitude, anger, and frustration. As you can see, it was quite a roller coaster. I have learned that the more intense you are, the more intense these experiences will be. Be gentle!

"Day 1 – Journal Notes

So many people are operating at a high wavelength. The key is to find people who are similar in energy and values and be with them to inspire one another. Anything we are willing to research in modern times, we will find. We have access to all the information in the world to create our own biases.

The vibration of the room was very high, but everyone was on their own journey. This may be a way people find God in the modern time. God gave us all the tools to have a direct relationship. We are technology. It feels like people are tired of being told what to do. They want to explore and learn for themselves. It is a delicate dance to find harmony because of tradition and modern evolution.

The breathwork blows my mind. Your body pauses your mind by only focusing on one thing. Why am I afraid to cry? Why is it so hard for me to cry? I had to pause my mind, and my body was excited to cry and purge those feelings. It was an organic recognition of the purest form of emotion.

Food – incredible! The food in Costa Rica is divine. Very few seasonings because the food is doing all the work. No added salt. I followed the instructions too fast and gave up coffee and alcohol. I cannot fathom how I would feel right now if my body was not working in my favor.

I am excited for tomorrow. Nervous because I am so far outside of my comfort zone. I look around and hear conversations. This seems to be true for most people. I keep telling myself, 'Fall back and be caught by the experience.' I have done my due diligence to know I am in a safe place to do this inner work. The only risk is missing out on this opportunity to grow and learn."

As I reflect on how this night changed my life, the biggest takeaway is remembering. We go through life, and it is so busy. We forget the intense moments that got us to where we are, such as the birth of our children. When my children were born, I was so scared. I felt completely out of control and had to surrender to the outcome. I was not giving birth. Men have the easy part of that process. Since I was so nervous and uncertain, it was almost like my mind wanted to forget.

Doing breathwork that night allowed me to go back and experience the joy of my children's births without fear. Madelyn is eight years old now. The day she was born, Shannon and I had NO clue what we were about to experience as new parents. Of course, it got easier with the birth of Quinn and Grayson, but it did not take away the fear of the unknown.

It was also eye-opening to not remember Grayson's birthday. I can look at pictures now, and they help a little bit. We had just moved into our new home, and my work life in June of 2019 was so intense that I was not fully in my body the day he was born. I was doing too many things at one time to operate at a high state of consciousness to experience the birth of my son. That does not mean I was not there physically.

This is one of my biggest lessons from that night. When life gets so busy you forget the most important things, it is time to slow down. This is a marathon, and there is no such thing as winning the race. Winning is being present and grateful for the moment in front of your eyes. Winning for me is now having the ability to REMEMBER!

Have you ever tried breathwork? I mean, you breathe every day! How many of those breaths are you conscious of? How often do you breathe deeply on purpose? There is magic in taking a hundred intentional breaths. Try breathing into your nose and out of your mouth a hundred times today, or you can set a timer for seven minutes. Take deep breaths with your eyes closed.

Our bodies make dimethyltryptamine DMT every day. DMT is also produced in many species of plants, often commonly used in indigenous Amazonian shamanic practices. It is one of the main active constituents of the drink ayahuasca. Ayahuasca is a vine and a flower mixed to create a large amount of DMT in your body. What I experienced quite literally mirrored people's records of dying and coming back. DMT is released in a massive wave when you take your last breath. Doing breathwork is a beautiful tool to create micro-experiences. The best part of breathwork is you can slow down and stop. This will stop the experience. Once you drink the ayahuasca, there is no turning back.

Do you know how it works? I had never done this before. When they told me I was going to breathe for 30 minutes, I had no idea what they were talking about. That first night opened my eyes to something unexpected. We breathe every day. It's part of our autonomic system. You sleep every night. You don't think about breathing when you're sleeping. We take breathing for granted. This was the first time I had been told how to breathe: how many times, how fast, and where to breathe from. I had to breathe only from my mouth. I thought I couldn't do this, that I was going to get thirsty. I was wrong.

How the breathwork is set up is critical. There was beautiful music in the background, and we breathed in and out of our mouths. It was the first time that I felt like I had intentionally breathed in a decade. Growing up, I had always been taught to breathe very well. I was a runner, a sprinter. Breathing through your nose is critical because the nasal cavity cleans the air so you can run faster. I understood this, but I had forgotten. When you stare at screens every day, you're not thinking about your breathing. When you're sitting at your desk, you're not thinking about your breathing. When you're driving your car, you're not thinking about your breathing. This night opened my eyes in such a beautiful way.

So, why does breathwork work? What is it doing? If you take a hundred deep breaths a day, in through your nose and out through your mouth, you will change the way your nervous system is working. Or you could set a timer for seven minutes. What happens to your body? Why does it? This is science. You can research this all day long. The beauty of breathwork is twofold. On the inhale, you increase the oxygen inside of your blood. And with the exhale, you remove the excess carbon dioxide from your body. When you do it in a very intense way, you activate all the parts of your cardiovascular system. But there's a miracle in our body; it's called DMT.

Science doesn't really know why this molecule exists in the human body. DMT is primarily created in our lungs. For thousands of years, DMT was more prevalent inside our bodies, and they actually call DMT the "spirit molecule." DMT creates a spiritual experience, a connection to something greater than you. Right now, our bodies are not making as much DMT as our ancestors' bodies did.

If you're like me, you will have to research all this stuff, find the science, and prove to yourself what DMT is doing. If you're a "trust the process" kind of person, just start breathing. DMT activates your pineal gland, which clears out the space in the front of your brain. This is where the creative force is inside of you. It is the most modern part of your brain, not where the fight-or-flight response resides. This is the part of your brain that has evolved past all of those archaic needs. Once I activated this part of my brain, I could not turn back. This night was the beginning of that activation. At the retreat I attended, they do the breathwork first so you can experience what it feels like to have DMT activated in your body prior to doing ayahuasca.

Ayahuasca is a vine that grows in the jungle. They boil the vine and mix it with a flower. Without that flower, that vine brew would not stay in your body because you would immediately throw it up. It is a miracle that they learned how to combine these thousands of years ago. What I will share with you in the next couple of chapters will not be for most of you. Activating DMT in your body for 6 to 12 hours in a row is a very intense experience. When you do breathwork, you're activating DMT on purpose in your mind for about 3 to 10 minutes. For most people, that is enough. For my wife, it is plenty. If you have an open mind about it, Google *"breathwork,"* watch YouTube videos on it, or go to a breathwork class in your area.

It's really fun to go on a date and do breathwork, but only with someone you really like. If you do, you will get to know each other better. If you are in a safe friend circle, breathwork could be a group activity. Instead of going to the bar or a movie, attend a breathwork session in your area. Have an open mind. Or go on YouTube and search "Wim Hof." This practice has been used since the beginning of humanity, especially in Eastern medicine, to help people solve major life traumas physically and emotionally.

I'm not a doctor, and I'm not an expert on breathwork. I am a user. That qualification allows me to impress upon you that it has been very helpful for my life experience. When my nervous system is not regulated, this is the first tool I turn to. I close my eyes and breathe in for five seconds, hold the breath for five, breathe out for five, and hold it out for another five before breathing in again. If you do that 15 times, you will immediately regulate your nervous system and your heart rate.

If you research professional athletes, you'll find that breathing is one of the major tools that they use to regulate and manage the intensity of their lives. Each of us has a different definition of intense. When my four-year-old is yelling at me, I feel like I drop into that intensity. I have two choices. I can yell at him, and I am very capable of doing that, or I can hold space for my four-year-old to understand why he is yelling. If I do the latter, I will stop any trauma from being passed down to him because I am able to manage my nervous system. Breath is a critical part of this evolution of your mind, body, and soul.

Some of you, as you read the next part of this book, will not have a desire to go to the depths that I went to. Even so, know that consistent breathwork practice can be a valuable tool.

CHAPTER 9

Night 2 – First Ayahuasca Ceremony

Where I went to do ayahuasca does a really good job of preparing you for what is to come. It is not a random trip to the jungle in the middle of nowhere and then hoping for the best. The setting is critical for feeling safe and letting this process play out nicely for your mind and body. There were shamans and medical doctors. There were people teaching classes every day. There is a process, and I believe it is critical to a successful understanding of medicine. Frankly, if I ever do it again, I will pick a more secluded place in the jungle, but this was perfect for my first experience.

When I woke up each day, I meditated and did my gratitude journal. I will share some of my notes.

"I am grateful for:

1. *Taking the risk to be here to work on my shadow self to better understand who I am today.*
2. *Modern times, which connect people and places. I am in Costa Rica with strangers from all over the world who are now friends.*
3. *Our life together as a family. We have so much fun together, and we have so many experiences.*
4. *A restful night of sleep to prepare for today.*
5. *God showed up in my breathwork.*

Here are a couple of points from my classes to prepare for the first night:

- *Pay attention to what feels wrong and explore it.*
- *What is coming is going. Turn towards the hard, knowing you are going to face it and remove it.*
- *The biggest gift in life is sovereignty.*
- *All addictions come from disease.*
- *Our souls know what we need, and sometimes, when we are not in alignment, we will feel completely disconnected from that inner voice.*
- *All growth comes from awareness during a forgetful period in life.*
- *This is happening for you, not to you.*
- *Setting intentions.*
- *Whatever you are seeing is leaving.*

Key questions if you get scared:

- *How is this making me feel?*
- *Do I feel this way in my life?*
- *When do I first recall feeling this way?*
- *Who have I become because of feeling this way?"*

I am very coachable. This started early on in my life. I would find people I wanted to mirror, and I would be a sponge. This has served me well. A couple of times, I was tethered to an individual who, in hindsight, was not right for my path. In general, though, I do a ton of research and then drop into the experience. That is what I did in preparing for ayahuasca. I researched every part of the experience and then surrendered. This retreat was completely outside of my comfort zone, so I embraced my surroundings and trusted them.

"Night 2 – Journal Notes (First Ceremony)

Intention – Show me who I have become.

Tonight, I went to the darkest place I have ever been. That was not where it started, though. I had pain in my heart for hours. I also had pressure in my temples. I fell asleep, and this put me into a very strange dream state. I dare say I was on the verge of death. My heart was sad, and I could feel the past trauma of my ancestors. I could feel that my heart needed to be healed. I had heard of sacred surgeries, but this was not something I believed in. It was as if something had happened that completely cleaned my heart. I awoke from this trance to purge. This was one of my fears of taking the medicine. It was so intense, and at the same time, it felt like I was releasing the stress and anxiety of the last few years in a couple of minutes.

I decided to go back up and get more medicine. I was scared, but I knew that it was part of the solution. After the second cup, I felt nothing different. I enjoyed the music, and I was in a deep meditation. I was at peace. I decided to go up again.

Shortly after the last cup of the night set in, I explored the scariest side of my mind I have ever witnessed. I saw what would happen to my mind and heart if I stayed on this current path. I saw myself becoming more depressed and sadder if I stayed on my current trajectory. I saw myself dying alone. I had chosen to pursue worldly financial success and, in the process, given up on my soul's mission. I started to get very sick, and I could not stop purging.

I cried out, 'God, please help me! I cannot do this alone.' In a flash, the feeling was gone. I stopped getting sick, and I got up and started walking. Then, my ego did a strange thing. It said, 'I got out of it.' The next second, I fell to the floor and started getting sick again. I cried out again, 'OK, OK, I get it! I am sorry! Please forgive me.'

Again, in a flash, the purging stopped, and peace came over my entire body. I was lying with my hand frozen in the open position. My hand lost its color as if I had died. Then I squeezed my hand and said, "You are alive!" I squeezed my hand as tightly as I could to feel the life go back into it. I was lying in the fetal position, praying for mercy and sharing how grateful I am to be married to Shannon and have three beautiful kids. I made a promise to God that I would follow my soul's mission from that day forward. At that moment, all I felt was a peaceful knowledge that this world and life are way more sophisticated than I could ever imagine.

Once the peace had settled in, the next part of the evening started. This was an open channel of information that I had never experienced. It felt like I was reading a book that was a shortcut to living a meaningful life. I lay on the ground, staring at the stars, and consumed 'downloads' for a period I cannot recall. At that moment, I felt like a newborn child in a 37-year-old body.

I started to hear my inner voice again, and it was sharing all the things I needed to help my family and myself. The voice was sharing a clear line of reasoning that I could not articulate after years of thinking through these very problems. I could hear exactly what I needed to say to Shannon and my mom, dad, and sister. The clarity from my inner self was like reading from a book.

Then I realized I was becoming a person I had chosen to walk away from. It was validating my choice to walk away. It showed me following that person into the exact life that I did not want to live. This moment of clarity caused me to cry uncontrollably. I had been second-guessing the choice I made to walk away from that person, and this moment showed me I had made the right call.

The last part of the night was very eye-opening. The lights had turned on, and because I took my last cup late, I was still deep in the medicine. The group was getting together to reflect on the evening, and I was by myself, purging into my bucket. It was not quiet, either. I looked up, feeling shame and embarrassment because of how loud I was, and the room was quiet. When I looked at the group, not one person was looking at me. This moment taught me that we are all on our own journeys. Do not get caught up in what other people are thinking of you. We are all so deep into our processes of life that it is best to stay in your lane."

Well, that was intense. I share these notes with great hesitation and with the knowledge that there is a lot to unpack. If you have spent time with anyone or done psychedelics yourself, you might simply say, "Par for the course." This was my first experience. It was like no course I had ever played, and there was no keeping score.

As I came out of the ceremony, I could not fathom what I had just gone through. I was in a state of total bliss, but at the same time, I felt like I had just experienced the scariest moment of my life. Talk about a paradox! The more people shared, the happier they were with the scary part. My mind was bending, and I wanted answers. Had I just paid money to be at a retreat to face this fear of dying, and now the fear was gone, but the trauma of the experience would stay with me for the rest of my life? How would I recover? Was this what I was supposed to experience? My mind still races when I think about that first night.

I have learned to be gentle and trust that my mind needed to go through this process to get out of the darkness I was sitting in. The medicine took it to an extreme to shake me out of the funk. I believe I had to be jolted out of the paradigm I was operating from to take it seriously.

It has been one year since this ceremony as I write this book. I am beyond grateful for the lessons from that night, and they have caused me to think differently every day since. The experience has also caused me to explore more of the human experience to understand how the mind works. The more answers I seek, the more questions I ask, creating an endless loop of curiosity.

I ask myself sometimes, *Am I better off after experiencing that evening?* My answer is always yes. Sometimes, I meditate and go back to that moment to relive what I went through. I am seeking new information for this current moment in life. My resolve is always to be present in this moment and this breath. Have gratitude for this day and every day. Breathe intentionally daily because, one day, you will take your last breath, and it might be by accident.

Some people tell me I am intense. I am intense because I have put myself in intense situations, some created by me and some for me. I believe I am designed to explore these moments because I am here to help others explore them as well. The more I learn, the more I can help others.

In moments like my ayahuasca experience, "die to live" starts to make all the sense in the world. Before this night, I thought I was in control. After that night, I realized the only thing I control is how I react to the world around me. I wake up every day with gratitude because I KNOW it is a miracle. I believe this evening was a gift for me to learn and understand how to move forward as a better man, husband, and father. I know I am better for running into the darkness of my mind and coming out the other side. I have mental bumps and bruises from it, and I am happy they are there.

I knew that I was experiencing a phase of hitting bottom. For some people, this is a quick process. For me, it was a culmination of events that started in August 2019, and the peak began on this night in February of 2023. That night, I talked to Shannon for a couple of hours. The ceremony ended at 3:00 a.m., and then we talked until sunrise at 5:30. I remember I could not wait for the sun to come up. I needed Father Sky in my life more than ever!

Have you had to experience the dark night of your soul? If yes, please write it down in a journal. You must remember the process for your current phase of life. I believe that when we are "going through the motions," we simply forget all the work we have done to get to that moment. If you have already explored the darkness and find yourself "going through the motions," you must remember you are going through the process to get you where you need to be. Everything is about remembering! Remembering hard times builds confidence and conviction to conquer current times. You have already found the answer for you; now you have to remember how you did it.

There is a phrase that is no longer allowed in our home: "I am BORED." When we humans are bored, we tend to do destructive things. We can fall into strange cycles of drinking, shopping, planning what's next, and so on. Everything I did when I was bored usually led to a mess that I had to clean up later. Now I say, "I am QUIET." This triggers an entirely different part of my brain. I want to seek peace and calm and be in the present moment. Whenever I am present, I can always find ways to entertain myself and my mind. Sometimes, this could be reading a book, taking a nap, or watching a movie with the kids. Being present in the moment has been my magic tool. What tools can you use to take the word BORED out of your mind and vocabulary?

If you have no experience with what I described above and are living in gratitude and present every day, you have already done the work. That does not mean something will not come up in the future that rocks your world. From this point forward, use this book as the reference point for when that happens. If you have not explored the darkness inside of you but feel like something is wrong with how you are going through life, this book might be the trigger.

Our minds are incredible, and they can purposefully forget the bad things that have shaped our current experience. If there is an underlying current of negative cycles in your life, finding the truth will give you your power back. Going through the motions is a symptom, not an outcome. If you find yourself wanting more all the time or are asking yourself, *Is this it?* You are at the beginning of the "waking up your higher self" process. Welcome to the river before the waterfall you will most likely go over. Start your safety training and embrace the hard work. The flip side is one of clarity. It is just the beginning, though!

For those of you who have used plant medicine or psychedelics, this might not seem so out of the ordinary. For those of you who have never experienced these types of altered states of consciousness, I'm sure my experience seems very intense to you. So, when we're thinking about how this medicine is working inside of our minds, we must take a step back and separate ourselves from what our mind was teaching us and what the reality of our situation is. Meditating on the lessons from the medicine is critical to the success of making heads or tails of what you experienced. My biggest takeaway from night one was that it's important to ask yourself, *Am I hearing a call? Is there something going on in my life or a feeling that I'm having? Does it keep coming up for me that there has to be more to this?*

I couldn't keep going through the motions every day. On the first night of the ayahuasca ceremonies, I learned who I had become and what track my life would follow if I stayed in my current mindset. You can read about the death of the ego or the darkness of the soul in many different psychology sources. Ego death means taking the part of your brain that is trying to control and manipulate your entire world experience and saying no thank you. It's the voice inside of your head that is constantly evaluating and describing everything. When we get rid of that voice, we enable ourselves to lock into a state of consciousness where we are fully present in the moment. When we are present in the moment, we stop fearing the future, and we stop getting depressed about the past.

If you are at a point in your life where you're feeling like you're going through the motions, like you're being called to something greater, you are already beginning this path to the new version of yourself. If you've already been through the dark night of the soul, you might have to go through it again as you upgrade or level up to a new state of awareness.

If you've never been through the dark night of the soul, it is a very intense experience. I have been through it a couple of times in my life. When my parents got divorced was a mini-version. I don't remember everything that happened. Then there was college, with breakups, decisions, or moments where I really had to explore myself to determine what version of me I wanted to be. I also had to go through a lot of dark nights of my soul when I was becoming a financial advisor. I would be up late at night, asking myself, "Is this worth it? Is all the pain, suffering, and rejection worth the outcome?"

There are moments in life when you succeed in overcoming these feelings of darkness, of your perception of your reality. These moments will forever change the trajectory of your life. The key lesson for me was that I had forgotten. I had forgotten the work I had done to get to this moment. I had forgotten the pain and suffering. I had become a numbed version of myself, a shell. This is not uncommon in the human experience.

So, if you're reading this and you're feeling the same way, embrace the feeling and have gratitude for acknowledging what you have done to get to this moment. If you've been through this darkness, write down those moments so you can remember how you got out. If this is the first time in your life where things aren't going exactly as you have planned, that's okay. Don't have any guilt. If you're reading this and were raised by amazing parents, grew up in a great house, have a great job, and everything up to this point has been really good, but you feel like you're going through the motions, that's okay.

I have talked to a lot of people in this circumstance. They feel like their problems are not worthy of exploration. It's easy for a person like me, who had difficult childhood circumstances, or people who have had a parent pass away prematurely, to drop into their trauma because it is so raw. It's been their reality, and they can use that extreme event as a catapult into their future. Obviously, they could do the opposite, too.

If you have had that great life, don't be afraid to acknowledge that the little things that aren't going right in your life are big things. Little things to someone else are big things to you, and that's okay. Write them down. This is the beginning of the search for the upgraded version of yourself. Going through the motions is a symptom. It is not the outcome.

Hearing the call to move into the new version of yourself is your intuition. For me, it's the acknowledgment of God asking me to do more. For you, it can be the universe, source or your inner voice. It doesn't matter what this is for you. If you're hearing it, pay attention. The louder it gets, the closer you are to the requirement of action to start moving into this new version of you.

CHAPTER 10

Night 3 - Second Ayahuasca Ceremony

As I waited to go back into the second night, I could not believe I was about to do this again on purpose.

"I must be crazy! Why would anyone do this? I just want to go home or hang out at the beach. Is this safe for my health? Can my body do this again? I have slept for 45 minutes in the last 24 hours. I have had almost no food because I have no appetite. This whole thing feels like a bad dream.

Notes from the day:

1. *Perhaps the anger inside of me is only partially mine.*
2. *Self-care requires spiritual practices.*
3. *Surrender to the how – the how is not for us to handle.*
4. *Language is critical for our mind to be clear on intentions.*
5. *Stop overthinking – let your heart lead your path, not the mind.*
6. *If you are aware, then you have a choice.*
7. *What is coming up right now that is triggering you? Why is that upsetting you?*
8. *Every time someone offers to help you, and you say no, you are saying no to the universe.*
9. *Build the muscle of self-love."*

"Night 3 – Journal Notes

Intention – Heal My Heart

What a different night! There was no intense drama or trauma. The main feeling was bliss and peace. There was a sense of knowing that I am exactly where I am supposed to be. I am doing the work I was designed to do. My job for the evening was to learn to breathe again. Deep and intentional breathing regulates the nervous system. I need to learn to breathe into the hard and stay calm. When I am angry, I have lost control of my nervous system. We are designed to control this. Be gentle. There are a lot of factors in the modern world that our nervous systems do not know how to handle. Technology is advancing so much faster than humans are evolving.

Tonight, I only had two cups. That is all I felt I needed and wanted. Tonight was all about my throat. I felt like a tube of toothpaste. There was negative energy in my body, and it ran from my feet all the way to my head. It felt like I was being rolled and squeezed to get every ounce of negative energy out of my body. The first time, it got stuck in my throat. The second time, some got stuck in my throat and the rest in my head. I started to cough violently, and I could not stop.

There was no purging with the first cup, so I went up to get a second. The toothpaste analogy was in full effect again. This time, when the energy got to my throat, I purged violently. I could feel the negative, dare I say, darkness coming out of my body. My voice felt different. My throat felt clean. My entire body felt clean. I had no desire to go up for another cup. I felt complete for the night, and I needed to rest.

Tonight, I was able to join the reflection. I was very aware and in a state of quiet reflection. I was observing and processing every part of other people's experiences. I felt honored to be in this room with all these people willing to do this work. The courage to do these two nights in a row is mind-blowing for me.

I have done hard things, and I cannot believe I am sitting here. I was so happy for them!

A few people were getting frustrated because they were fighting the medicine. Watching them spin out was a very valuable lesson. The more pressure they put on themselves and the situation, the more they resisted. I just wanted to give them a hug. I could feel the lesson for me. When things become intense, slow down and breathe. Do not get backed into a corner and fight your way out with a strategy. Surrender and trust that the corner is the lesson you need to learn. Force leads to destruction.

Lessons from the Evening:

1. Change *the word SHOULD to COULD for the rest of my life.*
2. *Being an overachiever has its place and time. Watching and resting does as well.*
3. *Feedback – be the light for people. Send them love and prayers for all the answers, for their own problems are within them.*
4. *When you walk through the darkness and into the light, it is easy to look back, knowing what the darkness looked like.*
5. *Patience is the most important part of the spiritual walk. Don't run, and don't set expectations to be results-oriented."*

When I look back at night two, I feel a little more "normal." To be clear, I do not believe in normal, but I remember how much I needed to feel less intense in that moment. The first night had spun me so far that I really needed to come back to some middle point. The toothpaste feeling still resonates with me to this day. I now know what it feels like to have a clean and clear throat.

Have you ever had that feeling where you could not talk? The quiver? I used to think that was nerves. Now, I know these moments require courage. These are the moments where my intuition needs me to vocalize something that does not land softly on the ears of the recipient. I now understand what it means to say, "Find my voice."

It is not always fun to say what needs to be said. I find there are times with my kids or wife that I know I need to share my mind and heart, but they do not want to hear it. This is usually when I'm setting a new boundary or following through on an existing one when I am tired. Now I know what the feeling is. This does not mean I always run at it at that moment. Most of the time, this feeling in my throat is coupled with anger. The best thing for me to do is take the things I know I need to say and say them later when I calm down. I am not perfect with this, and I still yell at my kids sometimes. Kids are good at triggering us parents! This awareness has been game-changing.

The next helpful reflection from night two that I think about daily is walking into the darkness. There are times when we must address the elephant in our mind. This pain, trauma, or loop might have been created by our actions or a circumstance outside of our control. We might be going through a death in the family, for example. In this darkness, we feel lost and isolated. We know the solution is to reach out, but that can feel almost impossible at that moment. I find that asking for help is one of the hardest things I do. It becomes harder when I feel my problem is not worth other people's time. Night two helped me to be gentler with myself.

Lesson one: change the word "should" to "could." I should wake up at five tomorrow. I should eat better food. I should be more present with my kids. I should stop staring at my iPhone so often. By changing "should" to "could," you immediately open up your psyche to look at the situation as an opportunity for evolution instead of giving something up. I could spend more time with my children. Right away, you're changing the paradigm for how you perceive that moment, and it's going to help you move in that direction.

If you're using the word "should" on a daily basis, start counting. I did this when I was learning to be a public speaker. I would count the number of times that I said "um," and it was not fun because it created internal criticism and doubt about the way I was speaking. When you start working on these types of specific details, there's going to be a process where you're very self-critical. Be gentle. It's part of the process.

Lesson two: being an overachiever has its place and time. Watching and resting does as well. I've been an overachiever and people-pleaser my entire life. It is part of my program. I love winning, and sometimes, that mindset forces me into situations where I'm not present for things that I need to be a part of.

For example, our lives are usually divided into personal, professional, and financial. In the personal category, we have our health and wellness, family, parenting and our dreams and passions. In our professional lives, we have goals and dreams, but they're more linear. They might be quarterly goals for production or sales. Then, obviously, all of these lead into our financial lives, which support all our personal goals.

I found it very hard to have all three of those things working in conjunction with one another. I was so focused professionally and financially when Shannon was a stay-at-home mom that I neglected my personal obligations. Health was a big one. I would eat in the most efficient way possible in the least amount of time possible, which led to burnout. The overachiever mindset eventually led to a destructive version of me. Then, I would step off and rest, rewarding myself by force. I would totally disconnect from the daily requirements for a month or a quarter just so I could recover mentally or physically.

The goal is to bring the three worlds into harmony, to do first things first, as Stephen Covey would say. I've discovered this harmony in my morning routine. These 30 minutes are required for my personal well-being. I need to get out of bed before my kids do. If I wake up to the children, I wake up with too much cortisol in my body because they usually jolt me out of bed, like when they have bad dreams in the middle of the night. So, that is a requirement for me to thrive.

To be in harmony, I also need to exercise. I love yoga, riding a bike, and hiking. I enjoy very intense yoga that challenges my mind and body. I also need to be conscious of my bedtime. The way you bookend the day defines it. So many people focus on what time they wake up in the morning. If you want to come into harmony with your life, focus on when you go to bed. Once you do, the rest will start to play itself out.

I am very intentional about getting to bed at 10 o'clock. Seven hours of sleep is my happy place. I will automatically get out of bed at five if I go to bed at 10, even without my alarm clock. These are just some things that I've come into harmony and balance with because the cycle of running really hard and being an overachiever creates a very challenging loop for everyone involved.

Lesson three: be the light for people. Send them love and prayers, for all the answers to their own problems are within them. For years, I've always been a fixer. As a financial advisor, I did this for 18 years. People would come to me, and their two main triggers were fear and money. They were delegating those two triggers to me as the financial planner because I managed people's fear of money. I was always trying to fix their problems. I loved helping others! I discovered I was taking on that energy and wasn't blocking it from my own life. This is probably one of the biggest reasons for my eventual desire to exit the financial services business as a financial advisor on a day-to-day basis.

When I work with people now as a coach, friend, father, son, or husband, my number one goal is to ask questions. If they come to me with problems, I cannot fix them. I can only come up with the right questions to help them elaborate in their minds the solution for their current circumstance. I can be a really good mirror for them. My whole life, people have told me how to fix my problems. I've had mentors who tried to help me shortcut processes by telling me what to do. Then, I would do the opposite because I hate being told what to do, where to be, or how to act.

This is particularly true now as my definition of Gratosis is sovereignty, ultimate freedom. This has been inside of me since I was a little boy. Now I'm just very clear on it. Knowing that my number one goal is sovereignty, why would I ever tell anyone else what to do? Treat people as you want to be treated. Respect other people's ability to come to their own life answers! People are going to ask you for help all the time. If you want to grow and strengthen your relationship, reflect their questions back to them. Keep doing that until they light up in the recognition of their own solution to their problem.

Lesson four: when you walk through the darkness and into the light, it's easy to look back, knowing what the darkness looked like. This is a beautiful gift of plant medicine. It opened up a tunnel for me to see the light on the other side. I could see my divine purpose. It's a gift, but then that tunnel closes. You come back to the present, and you have a flashlight showing 30 to 40 feet in front of you. We then commit to one step at a time, one breath at a time, and one day at a time.

The beauty of doing inner work, shadow work, is that it helps you come into balance with your purpose. This will begin your evolution into your best version of yourself. It is not going to be easy, and you're not going to have all the answers. The gift of being able to walk through the darkness is that you can see what not to do in the future. You can write down and reflect on all your mistakes, behaviors, and feelings. You can have gratitude for that part of your journey, and you can use it as the light for your future steps.

We have all heard that "hindsight is 20/20." The adage rolls off people's tongues all the time. When I hear this, I often feel like it disregards the pain that someone had to walk through to learn the lesson. The lesson above helps me to be more compassionate to myself and others.

I chose to walk through the darkness on night one. That is an interesting thing about the work in ayahuasca. I had the opportunity to face my fear and see who I had become. I could have taken an easier path and ignored my truth. Night two gave me a deep sense of gratitude for myself and my willingness to walk into the darkness of my soul and address what was coming up. I was scared, but it absolutely needed to happen. The light on the other side of the tunnel is more valuable and bright now knowing the choices I made for myself to explore the process of being on the other side.

Looking back, I feel like I would have had a different outcome if I had stopped at night two. I felt complete in the circle of healing. Little did I know that this was just the beginning of what would transpire over the next two ceremonies. Unfortunately, and fortunately, this was just the tip of the iceberg.

Lesson five: patience is the most important part of the spiritual walk. Don't run, and don't set expectations. This lesson was very hard for me. I am a stubborn, overachieving human. I love running. I love setting very high expectations for myself, and I love vision planning and focusing on results. This type of work is very different from setting a sales target, which is a linear exercise where you can use math, numbers, and behavior.

On this walk, do you find yourself becoming more self-critical? Has your standard of life increased so much that you have forgotten how to be kind to yourself? I am often tempted to fall back into this trap.

Here's an easy example. When I drink the correct amount of water for my body every day, I am a hundred percent happier. Some days, I do not drink enough water. On those days, I ask myself, *What is your problem? Why can't you just drink water?* We know we are all very harsh on ourselves. Or I can say, *I am going to drink a glass of water now. Tomorrow, I will set up my environment better to accomplish drinking the correct amount of water.*

We must be patient with ourselves. Being so allows us to be patient with others. The more we embrace the idea that people are doing the best they can, the more kindness will prevail! Is there anything in your life that you know makes you your very best? Write it down in your journal. Every day you do it, make that your first point of gratitude. For example, I might write, "*I am grateful that I consumed enough water today. I can feel the positive impact of hydration in every aspect of my physical and emotional body.*"

As you start this spiritual opening and walk, you might feel confused because the answers to what you need to do are not coming through. Sometimes, the answer is to just sit. My favorite analogy for this is to think of a tree swing hanging from a tree in a beautiful field. Sometimes, when you're sitting on that swing, the entire earth pivots under your feet. It is your job to just enjoy the view. Your intuition will tell you when to jump off the swing and get back into motion. Trust the universe or God. Trust that pieces have to be moved for the next phase of your life to be unraveled. And don't forget to enjoy the view.

CHAPTER 11

Night 4 – Third Ayahuasca Ceremony

"We are about to enter a time in history where more people will be lost than guided by their intuition. This is not being done to us, but for us to end cycles. For those with a plan, this will not be easy, but it will be a time for breakthroughs. Those without a plan will need to create one, or they will be lost in other people's intentions.

The most important step in maintaining this state of clarity on consciousness is practice. I must use the daily practices I have already implemented, but now they will become more advanced. This is the only way to take what I learn in theory and bring it into my living reality. If we are not in practice, we will revert to our old ways.

Half of the work is explored IN the medicine.

Half is integrated when we return home.

The medicine will stay in our bodies for 30 days. When we leave here, we will have a clean and clear slate to rebuild from."

"Ayahuasca Night 3 – Intentions and Pre-Thought:

Tonight, I am excited to go deep within. I am nervous that I did not go through enough pain on night one. I have faith, and I am focused on what needs to be revealed to me. I have a more intense focus for tonight compared to the relaxed mindset of last night.

My Intention: Show ME the way to walk hand in hand in every aspect of life with Shannon."

I am not going to share all my notes from Night 3 because this night revolved around my parents, and I do not want to share their story. This is my book. However, I will share a little bit to help with this part of the story.

My parents made very hard choices at a young age. They chose to follow through and have their first child. They got married and built a home. Then they had me. I remember the day my mom, sister and I left my dad. I was seven. I cannot imagine the pain my parents went through to get to that point.

In the medicine, I was able to fall into that moment and look into their eyes as my 37-year-old self. I felt more compassion and empathy for them than I had ever felt before. A realization struck me: *They were doing the ABSOLUTE BEST they could possibly do in the circumstance they were in.* A wave of peace came over me, and I forgave them for everything, both the things I remembered and anything I had forgotten. Not only would I go home with a clean slate, but they would now have a clean slate with me.

"Night 3 – Journal Ceremony Notes

There will be miracles! Everything is a miracle. The fact that we live on this rock in the middle of an infinite universe that is EXPANDING is amazing. Tonight, I had to battle the feeling that I was not worthy of love. Everything about this night was divinely feminine. The night started calmly with the recognition of my parents' divorce. Once I moved through that, the experience got more chaotic.

With the second cup, I accessed a different 'world.' I moved into a spiritual realm. It felt like I was walking into the light, almost like what people describe in near-death experiences. I was not scared and wanted to keep walking towards it. The closer I got, the more my body started shaking uncontrollably. Then I heard a voice: 'You are too close. Go back down.' I got scared because I did not know what I was accessing or where I was. Then I started taking deep breaths and came back to my physical body.

After purging all those thoughts, I felt more centered and in awe. Once this feeling came over me, a stream of consciousness filled my head. What came through was that I had to start writing diagrams immediately in my journal. Everything on the planet operates in frequencies and vibrations. The oldest game in humanity is the battle between good and evil. Both light and dark warriors use the exact same frequencies and energy for their cause. It is a flip of the same coin.

We are at a time in history when evil is at 49% and good is at 51%. The scale must be tipped, or sadly, there will be so much pain and destruction. I also felt a clear knowing that the scale will NOT tip. Good will again prevail, and this journey in medicine is the beginning of that understanding.

Millions of people around the world are questioning just like I was, which led me here to Costa Rica. The miracle of our existence is meant to be felt by every person on earth. This does not mean pain and suffering will disappear, but we can start moving in the direction of love and kindness for every soul on this planet.

I felt all these frequencies. I felt like a student in a classroom learning how to feel the world. In feeling frequencies, I was learning how to walk next to the good and avoid the bad. I felt no need to judge the bad because that is not my job. My job is to understand the bad so I can be aware and avoid traps that could send me off course. I also learned how to know the difference between my ego and my intuition. My EGO comes through SLOWLY. It does not know exactly how to process information, so it builds a story. My EGO really likes fear and urgency. My intuition is fast, fast, fast, and also very calm. It is more of an instant knowing than story building or creating."

This night was very interesting because it moved me from learning that I am worthy of the love of my parents, wife, and children to the collective consciousness of the world as a whole. I will reflect on part one first, as it feels very simple compared to part two.

The biggest lesson I learned on night three was that I am worthy to ask for help, and I am worthy of my family's love. Since my parents' divorce when I was young, I have always found myself growing up very fast. I was seven when I had single parents. They had to work hard and pay the bills. I would live 55% of the time with my mom and 45% of the time with my dad. I lived out of a suitcase during that time, almost until I was in college. I lived with my grandparents for a good part of the summer and fished almost every day with my grandfather.

I was always on the move, so getting my driver's license felt like a miracle. Then I could go anywhere I wanted with my backpack and some good tunes in my 1997 Jeep Wrangler. With all this independence, I learned to build a beautiful life for myself and my family. I learned at a young age to make money, and because I was always an old soul, people would ask me for help. I believe the best salespeople in the world create a safe place for their clients to ask questions and ask for help. Quite the paradox is that I could create that space for others, but I was not able to do that for myself.

Night three taught me that ALL PAIN in life comes from REJECTION. Every time someone tries to help me, I reject them and, therefore, cause them pain. People who offer help want to help. Through receiving help, we receive the gift of their love. I believe God works this way, too! I am grateful for learning to accept love from my family and friends. It has and will make my life so much better and more fun. It also helps to be conscious of my children asking for help. The more they ask, the safer they feel. We all want to feel safe and avoid rejection. Humans do WILD things in the quest for the first and avoidance of the second.

Observe yourself. One of the most common human choices when we get rejected is self-isolation. This is a very sad place in our minds. We get stuck here. We feel it would be easier to watch Netflix than face the rejection. The more you pay attention to how people reject you and how you reject others, the faster you will build your relationships.

Shannon and I have done a ton of work on this. We run so hard and fast as a married couple with three little kids that, sometimes, we will say something crass or quick because we're in the middle of getting the kids ready or jumping between conference calls. The lack of acknowledgment is a rejection. If you look in people's eyes when you reject them, they will look away. Eye contact is critical to understand how people are feeling around you. Pay attention to what people do as you're talking to them. If they keep looking away, they are uncomfortable. They don't feel safe.

It's not your fault all the time. You could be triggering them due to something that happened to them a decade ago. Understanding how to communicate with other humans has been the gift of my life, and it's helped me build every business, relationship, and sales transaction. Work hard to make eye contact with other people. I'm not talking about staring at them. Use productive eye contact to evaluate how people are feeling being around you, and then pay attention to yourself. If someone is talking to you and you keep looking up and away, to the side, or down at the ground, it's a sign that you are feeling uncomfortable.

The second part of the night was about good over evil and the collective consciousness. I will not speak too much about this because I do not know exactly why I learned it. It is possible I was watching too much news, and all the fear was embedded in my mind. Perhaps it all just needed to be purged out.

One major validation was my mission with The Motion of Gratitude. It is an important time in history to help change the focus to good. Gratitude has been the hardest thing for me to sell. I sold sporting goods. That was easy because kids needed a lot of gear. I sold life insurance. That felt easy, too. Most people are scared to die. I sold investments. That was a little harder, but most people are confused by all the products in the financial service industry. Selling gratitude for under a hundred dollars is quite the opposite. People believe it is too simple, "there must be more." No matter how much rejection I face, this is now my life's work!

The second part of the evening increased my conviction about why I must keep going. In the end, the experience was very intense, and I wrestled with the darkness in parts of the world and circles of people. I choose to do good and be a candle in the room. I will shine brightly whether the lights are on or off. It is the only thing I can control!

Here are some questions from the first part of the night to ask yourself: Who is rejecting you right now that is causing you pain? Who are you rejecting right now that is causing them pain? Are these relationships worthy of repair? If yes, are you able to move forward without external intervention? If the answer is no, ASK for help! If the answer is yes, repair the relationship. Are you role-playing this resolution with a third party with no affiliation to the other person? Once you role-play and have a plan, when will you call that person? The faster you can clear this, the better your life will be.

We all hurt people by accident and sometimes on purpose. I have found that in almost every case, this is due to poor communication. Words matter, and delivery is EVERYTHING! Work with a coach to help you formulate resolution. If you have the right coach, they will ask you questions until you have discovered your OWN answers. We are the problem and the solution.

This fact is not always fun to think about, but it is true. Take this feedback with a grain of salt.

A second exercise. Are you a candle in a lighted and dark room? If your light blew out, are you willing to face the reason? Are you using gray energy to move your agenda? Manipulation is an example. I am being gentle here because there are agenda-selling models. The younger we are, the easier it is to not know you are selling someone else's agenda. When you think about the dark, do not think you are evil. Our minds have two parts: the three-year-old who wants to do whatever he wants and the wise sage who knows you should not eat ice cream every night.

I felt like my candle had been blown out. No matter what circumstance I was in, I could not see the beauty of the outcome. Your light will go out. It is part of this journey. Failure is growth. My awareness now focuses on how fast I can relight my candle. Accepting that your candle is going to blow out will help you to be gentle with your story. Your tools will be different from mine. Find them. Find out what your definition of Gratosis is, and then use the tools you've learned from this book to maintain that state of consciousness.

Be gentle with yourself here. I have sold things to pay my mortgage that were good for the client but sped up by my agenda. Financial need is a driving reality in our lives. We all are chasing safety and avoiding rejection. If you are feeling out of alignment, ask yourself, "Do I want to fix it?" If the answer is yes, YOU are DOING IT already. KEEP GOING!

Change is not going to come overnight. These are hard skills to master, requiring an elevated state of consciousness. Maintaining the required level of focus takes work, awareness, and intention, and you will not always want to do it. I don't always want to do it. I work hard to be fully engaged in my mind and body when I am with others, but I am human. I get tired! When this happens, I take a break. I go and sit outside. I take my shoes off. I lie on my back in the grass. I reset so people know I want to be with them. Every interaction deserves this level of awareness. Your moment with the person across from you might change the rest of their lives!

Sometimes, I will take a break from everyone and everything. I'm resetting my nervous system. Every time I reject someone, lose my patience, or get angry, it's because I'm operating with low energy. I feel tired, frustrated, and frantic. No one is perfect in these moments. Instead of doubling down and continuing to do the things you think you should be doing, just stop.

That was one of the most beautiful aspects of living in Costa Rica. You cannot go fast there. The faster you go, the more frustrated you become. The dirt roads, if you drive fast, will break your car. If you break your car, you cannot find a mechanic to fix it. Therefore, you messed up your entire life rhythm because you were careless. Sometimes, we just need to slow down. In that time, reflect on what you did to get your nervous system out of whack and just keep learning.

If you're rejecting someone and they are rejecting you in a constant cycle of pain, is it worth staying in that relationship? Some relationships are non-negotiable. I choose every day to step into the hardness of having children. My relationships with my children are so worthwhile to me that I would do anything to consistently not reject my children. I would do anything to consistently not reject Shannon. All of these relationships are part of my journey of life, and they are non-negotiable.

Some relationships, though, are not required. As you walk into this new version of yourself, dare I say upgrade or evolve, there will be relationships in your life with acquaintances or friends who are not going to understand what you're doing. They are going to reject you. When this happens, you have to ask yourself, *Will they ever understand who I'm becoming?* If you feel in your heart and intuition that the answer is no, you need to create a barrier between your psyche and their opinion. If you cannot create that barrier, you are going to have to walk away. That doesn't mean forever, though.

When I was young, I used to think relationships were either yes or no. We were going to be either friends now and forever or never friends at all. People I coached a decade ago are coming back into my life. We picked up right where we left off. Obviously, we evolved and changed over that decade, but it is amazing to pick up the phone and experience each other for who we are today and find the beauty in how we crossed paths before and are now doing it again.

Nothing is permanent. Everyone is on this journey. Everyone will come into a higher state of consciousness at some point because we all die. Through the dying process, we are forced into this understanding. If people around you are not supporting this walk, do not burn the bridge. Just put a "closed" sign up. You're likely going to take that sign down in the future. The more you can learn not to burn bridges, the more beautiful the serendipity will be for the rest of your life.

The last point on this is that sometimes, you need third-party intervention. If you're in a relationship that's necessary and desired, don't be afraid to bring in a third party to help you navigate conflicts. Do not have triangular conversations behind peoples' backs. The triangle has to be inside the same room. If you use the third-party mediator as a go-between, a lot will get lost in translation, and nine times out of 10, the conflict causing the disruption will be avoided because everyone wants to avoid conflict. Get yourselves in the same room.

Set ground rules. If the relationship is worthy of being fixed, the first ground rule is to say, "I love you. My intention is not to destroy you in an effort to solve this problem." Once this is your number one ground rule, you can proceed with caution and have a really beautiful conversation about the turmoil, the disruption, and how to move forward from it. Everything comes back to love and kindness. Use that as the foundation for conflict resolution. And at the end of the conflict, hug it out. You're not going to agree on everything. Humans don't agree on everything. There's a reason there are a hundred different cereal boxes in the cereal aisle and they all get purchased. The goal is not one hundred percent alignment; the goal is productive unity to move forward.

Every morning, when I come out of my meditation, I need to be clean and clear. I think about the day before. Did I hurt anyone by accident? Did I yell at one of the kids because I was at my wit's end? It was nine o'clock at night, and they were not going to bed. The only way for me to come out clean and clear from those meditations is to acknowledge if I did something wrong the day before and then go and talk to the person I wronged.

The hardest mountain for me to climb right now is being a father, so nine times out of 10, the person I've wronged is one of my children. I'll start my day with, "Hey, bud, I'm sorry that I lost my patience with you at bedtime last night. I know you were just trying to feel safe and fall asleep. I was exhausted, and I couldn't maintain patience with you. I love you."

The faster we learn to repair relationships, the faster we turn other people's lights back on. We can light their candles by repairing the damage as fast as possible. When I look into another person's eyes, I know if their light is shining. This is a process. It's not perfect. But awareness of your light and the light of others is the beginning of a beautiful reset of how you move forward in your relationships.

CHAPTER 12

Night 5 – Fourth Ayahuasca Ceremony

By this point in the week, I was running on low sleep and using my days to sit in quiet and listen to music. I had almost no appetite. I had purged all the bad stuff out of me. I was feeling the cleanest and clearest, physically and mentally, I have ever felt. After three nights, I had no idea how to handle night four. This next ceremony would last 16 hours instead of 10. The only thing I could wrap my head around was my intention.

Show me WHO I am to become and trust.

In hindsight, this was NOT a good intention. It was too open and sophisticated for my level of experience in medicine work. Now I know, and I will not set a "future self" intention. Too many things shift every day to know the future. Asking my mind to go through this exercise was torture. I believe I set myself up poorly for this ceremony, and that is why it was and is still a traumatic moment in my life. I also know it was needed for my process. Caution: in the work, you might break something that will require MORE work.

"Ceremony Four Journal Notes:

That was quite the journey. We took a stronger brew tonight, a Columbian one. I could barely keep the medicine down. After I took the medicine, I meditated. It was very calm. Perhaps I had been overreacting to the hype around the ceremony. This could not have been further from the truth. This was the calm before the storm of cups two and three. What followed was hours of pain in the same loop. I kept experiencing death and rebirth cycles. People have talked about this before, feeling this energy. I never knew what they were talking about. Now I do, and I hope I never have to experience it again.

I went up to get my third cup, and I was angry. Why was this 'medicine' making me live this horrible loop, and why did it convince me that the only way through was another cup? I was only up there because I was stubborn to the idea of failure. In hindsight, that was not the right thinking for this night. The battle of death and rebirth continued. It was like I could not surrender to this reality of the life cycle. I knew I had to die to live again, but I was too scared to feel that feeling again. This was one of the most humbling moments of my life. I needed help, and I did not know how to get it.

Finally, we broke off into small healing circles. This was the most profound moment of my adult life. The shamans raised my vibration, and my entire body started shaking and vibrating, very similar to last night when I got too close to that bright light. Then I purged more than any other night before. It was as if the negative energy was exiting every cell in my body. It was intense, and when I stopped, I felt cleaner and clearer than I had ever felt in my life. I was 'reborn.' This is the only way I can describe it. It felt like I was a newborn child in a 37-year-old body.

I also learned about the fun of my spirit animal. I am a spotted black jaguar. We are all connected: plants, animals, every human. We are all in this together! I did not believe in any of this before this day. I still do not know where it all fits. I do know what I felt and saw, though. It might take me years to make sense of all of this.

I got up and walked outside. I was still deep in the medicine. The sun was coming up. I sat next to my friend, and we started laughing uncontrollably. He was like a newborn, too. He is similar to my age. I saw him as a cobra and shared that I was a jaguar. Then we giggled like we were in third grade. It was the most playful I had been in years.

Things took a turn from there, though. I had a sudden flash of my deathbed. I saw Shannon and the kids at my current age, having to take me off life support. I'd had a heart attack and could not bring myself back. At that moment, I could not understand if I was in the medicine anymore. I thought I had actually died and was in heaven. I cried and begged God for mercy. 'Why did this have to happen? I want to go back to my family. PLEASE!' Then I thought I was in purgatory and was going to have to do these ceremonies every day until I made up for my sins. Next, I saw myself at my funeral. I saw Shannon and the kids at their current ages. I saw the pain in their eyes. I saw Shannon having to raise our children ALONE. I was devastated.

One of the shamans came over to help me. He walked with me over to a bench. We sat down, and he stared deep into my eyes. He asked, 'Do you see this pain and fear coming up in my life?' I said I did.

We talked through the fear, and he said, 'The past is gone. The future is unknown. Be gentle, brother. You are going through a process.'

I dropped into absolute bliss. I looked up at the sun. I felt God shining on me. My faith was restored, and I knew this entire existence was on purpose. This moment will change the rest of my life. I was reborn into a higher state of consciousness. There is no turning back to my old life after this."

You have just seen the most vulnerable side of my soul, and you are probably saying, "Wow, that was intense." And it was. I promise. I hadn't cried that much ever in my life. I had not felt that much pain ever in my life. Some days, it's hard to understand what happened that evening. It was almost a year ago now. Sometimes, I feel like I have PTSD. Watching yourself die at the age that you're currently at is really intense.

This is the interesting thing about DMT. When you take your last breath, your pineal gland gives you a massive shot of the compound. This is to remove the fear of dying and remind you that you are going home. Just before people take their last breath, they might talk about seeing family members in the corner of the room. They might talk about seeing a light. They might say they're talking to relatives. I have been with people in the last days of their lives, but I've never held someone's hand at their last breath.

The only way I've been able to put this night into perspective has been to research the experience. Reading and watching accounts of people who have died and come back helped me figure out how to stabilize myself and put what happened in a framework that my psyche could grasp. As you research DMT, you'll discover that this is what the compound is for. The intensity of your experience depends on how much ayahuasca you drink.

This event presented the biggest paradox that we all explore: die to live. Growing up Catholic, I understood this from a Christian viewpoint. Now, a year after my ayahuasca experience, I can see that I had to go through the death and rebirth of my soul to be the man I am today. It was a gift to die, and I got to experience the love of my wife and the love of my children. The plant medicine taught me how much they love me. How much they need me. I had convinced myself prior to that day that maybe they were better off without me. My soul is here for a reason. I needed to remember!

These are dark thoughts, and the heart attack I experienced during this ayahuasca journey rocked me. Perhaps this was my soul's way of giving up but doing it with integrity. I could return to heaven, and my wife and kids would have money from my life insurance. They would be better off with the money than me. I think many people have been somewhere near here in their own minds. Or perhaps I am alone on this one. What I lived through that night was a miracle that I don't want to ever experience again.

I learned that the more closed you are, the bigger the opening is. I had become very closed. I had become very isolated. I was the problem, and I *am* the solution. Receiving this wake-up call was the most beautiful thing I could have experienced at that juncture of my life. It proved to me that I was the solution, but I could not neglect the problem. That night saved me! People say that when you do ayahuasca, it's like doing ten years of therapy in a week. I can honestly say that's how it felt for me. The things I learned over those four nights were what I had been ignoring for the last four years.

Everything that we've been through with COVID, the isolation and the rejection, all of it, came up and out. We've all been going through this for the last four years. We cannot brush any of it under the rug. It has to be addressed. We all have to come together as one, in loving kindness, to understand that the isolation, quarantining, and fear changed us, our children, and our relationships. That night, it became clear to me that my depressing thoughts were no longer worth having because every day is a miracle.

This doesn't mean I don't have hard days. I am still building a company. My website still gets hacked periodically. I still have technology issues. I still have parental issues. My children still fight. Shannon and I still have disagreements. These are all practical, real things that happen in life. What I learned that evening was to not attach to them, to separate myself from those situations. I love my wife, I love my children, and they love me. So, whenever I get frustrated or angry, I say, "This is not worthy of me spiraling down. Come back to neutral." Life is a miracle. Spiral up or stay neutral.

Take what I'm saying and use it for good. I also challenge you to do some research on near-death experiences. Why am I fascinated by this research? For me, it's the commonality of what people share. Whenever I'm researching anything, I think of the similarities between people's experiences. If hundreds of people are experiencing the same thing, is it because of a collective consciousness, or did they actually experience it? For me, there are so many similarities between what I experienced and the accounts of others that I cannot pretend that it was not real.

Accounts of near-death experiences go back 50, 70, 80 years, many written by doctors and psychologists. That's why I discount the idea that a collective consciousness causes the similarities. This consciousness comes from your environment, so you would have to be around other people to share their biases. These people, however, came from different generations yet had very similar experiences. Whatever the answer, we will all continue to question why we are here and what happens when we leave our bodies. These are very powerful questions that have been asked since the beginning of time.

What I experienced that night helps me to know that there's something, and it helps me to know that I have to be a good person. I have to love and care for others. I have to help children on earth. A massive sadness has risen in our world, and we have two choices when it comes to dealing with it. We can choose to ignore it and say it's too late, or we can say that if we have to experience this darkness, then it means we are meant to. We can chalk it up as a loss, or we can go on offense. We can be the light in the dark room. We can love people who need our love and support. We can feed people who are going through very hard times. We can address the mental health crisis in the world. We can all come together and say, "Enough is enough."

Let's start focusing on what really matters: the human experience. We all need to eat, sleep, and go to the bathroom. Think about what a baby needs. If you can take those same needs and apply them to yourself, no matter how old you are, you will win. A baby needs food, to go to the bathroom, to sleep, and, most importantly, to feel safe. The baby needs love. The mother's love. The father's love.

I believe a mothers' intuition is the most important part of human progression. We all need our mothers. If your mother is not a part of your life, you need this intuition from another source. I believe this is the purest form of love we can encounter on this planet. We need to embrace mothers' intuition as a society right now. Mothers will always want what's best for everyone on this planet, and we all have a mother.

That night brought me into a state of consciousness where I love people so much. When I see someone in pain, I want to be part of the solution. And quite often, that solution is free. You can smile at someone and change their entire day. You can help someone laugh. The average seven-year-old laughs three hundred times a day. The average adult laughs 50 times a day. Laughing is medicine. Levity is beautiful.

We're in a very challenging time in history, but it can be the beginning of a beautiful future if we make it that way. We must go on offense and choose to step into the solution of caring and loving. The beauty of doing plant medicine is that it teaches us we are all one. Treat everyone as you would want to be treated. At their cores, every religion or spiritual practice teaches the same thing, be it Buddhism or Catholicism. The golden rule is to treat others as you want to be treated. Breathe into every interaction in your day. Leave everyone better than you found them. In life, there is rejection, isolation, and conflict. If those three things are part of your experience right now, acknowledge them and breathe into them.

I'm going to share a couple of comments on psychedelics because I don't want to put them on a pedestal. Ayahuasca was my tool. Everything you learn in medicine is you. The medicine intensifies your human experience. That extreme is necessary to teach you quickly. I am an intense person. This is an intense part of the book. The level of intensity that I needed to go through to get into this state of knowing is because of me, of who I am.

Please do not read this and say, "Man, I should go do ayahuasca." I needed a very intentional process to get to this moment. I researched ayahuasca for five years. I meditated, journaled, and focused on my mental and physical well-being for the three years leading up to taking it. I was deeply in the river of The Motion of Gratitude. I had gotten to a dark spot, and I needed a waterfall. To be honest, I had no idea how intense it was going to be. Tread lightly with this tool. As more plant medicine gets legalized in America and around the world, people are going to become attached to the idea of doing this as part of a trend. Please do not do that. Do not take psilocybin or ayahuasca and go to a family picnic. Do not take this medicine recreationally if you are seeking to do healing work. It will not work. It will drop you into very scary circumstances.

Everything about this work is based on mindset and setting. If you are not in a setting that is nature-based, clean, and clear, you're setting yourself up for failure. If you are not around people who understand how the process works, who can hold space for you, who can feel your feelings and be in it with you, do not do this. Do not take mushrooms for the first time by yourself and sit in your house. This medicine has been used for thousands and thousands of years, and it's been used in a very traditional sense by shamans and medicine people. It requires a massive amount of understanding.

This is the number one lesson for this part of the book. I did not share this most intimate experience of my life to encourage you to mirror it. I shared it because we all go through this experience at some point, and I want you to know how I put my life back together. I want my story to be a resource for people who have done this type of work and have fallen apart. This needs to be taken seriously.

The question I have for you is, "Do you wake up every morning and say happy birthday to yourself?" That is my number one takeaway from doing plant medicine. Every morning, I wake up, watch the sunrise, and thank God for another day to do good things. I still celebrate my birthday on July 9. I still go through the motions of the traditional birthday celebration: the cake and the candles. I don't do it for me. I celebrate my birthday every day. I work hard to acknowledge that on that night in February of 2023, I had to die to live. And I choose to live daily because I don't take life for granted, and I know how fast this trip is on this planet.

Everyone comes here as a 10 out of 10. I believe in God, and I believe he built us that way. But then life throws us curve balls. We might come to a place where we're a five out of 10. Learn how to find the tools to get you to be a 10 out of 10 again. The tools are inside of you. I didn't know how to find them. Even though I had been meditating and gratitude journaling, I had lost sight of where to find the beauty inside of my human experience. Therefore, I took the extreme measure of going to Costa Rica to do ayahuasca. I am so grateful for that experience.

As our society moves into this open-minded time in history, we must have caution. This medicine is used to cure diseases of the body and mind. It is meant to be taken and then left behind. It is a tool in the toolbox. It is not the primary tool. I believe it is meant to be used and then removed after the solution presents itself.

The beauty of mushrooms and ayahuasca, for most, is non-addictive. The work is so hard that people do not want to keep coming back for more. Integration is the most important part of this process. The more you open yourself, the more you have to integrate. The more you learn, the more you have to manage. If you've already started this exploration, I'm excited for you, but I also want you to breathe into whether you are integrating all of the information that you've already obtained.

In the next part of this book, we will go into integration and the tools that can help you achieve it. I will also share how I put my life back together, unwinding 37 years of me to create a new and exciting version of myself.

PART 3

Integration

CHAPTER 13

Physical Change

In February 2023, I left Costa Rica and flew back to America. As anyone who's gone to this type of retreat knows, this can be a very jarring experience. In this third part of the book, I will explain everything I did and continue to do to integrate the information I learned. The information is in three parts. Part one is about physically integrating the things I learned. Part two is about the mental side of the integration. What did I have to do on a day-to-day spiritual practice to maintain my awareness of what I had learned? The third part answers the question, where are we going? I will share what I learned and how my family and I are going to implement it in this part of our journey, personally, professionally, and financially.

Let's jump into the physical. I flew back to the United States and landed in Houston, Texas. Costa Rica is a very kind, loving culture. Though one of the poorest countries in the world, it's also one of the happiest. At the airport in Liberia, everyone's smiling, and the service is very kind and loving. The Houston airport, on the other hand, or any major airport in America, is gigantic. Keep in mind that the medicine stays in your system for 21 to 30 days. I was still deeply in the medicine when I landed in Houston. When I got off that plane, I stepped into a world I was not ready for. The speed was so fast. I kept looking at people, and no one was looking at me. It was jarring. I had learned to maintain and sustain eye contact in that brief time, but I couldn't make eye contact with anyone.

From Houston, I flew to Orlando, Florida. My family was wintering in Central Florida. Orlando airport is just as huge and busy as Houston's. It was midnight when I landed. My Uber was canceled. I didn't know how I would get to my RV, which was an hour and a half away. Again, still on the medicine, I texted Shannon, telling her I didn't know what to do. She couldn't come to pick me up at the airport because she had three little kids sleeping in our RV. I went outside to look for a cab. A Nigerian man was there, and when we made eye contact, he knew I needed him. He said, "Hey, brother, do you need help?"

I want to cry when I think about his eyes. He knew something that I knew. He had been through something similar to what I had gone through. I didn't know this man. I said, "I need to get to Auburndale."

"That is pretty far away," he said. "I won't be able to get a ride back."

"How much is it to get to Auburndale?" I asked him. When he told me it would be $150, I offered to double the fare to compensate him for his drive back to Orlando.

He safely got me to the RV park. You have to imagine how I felt at that moment. Three days prior, I had thought that I had died. When he dropped me off, he shook my hand and said, "It's nice to meet you, brother." Such terms as "brother" and "sister" were common at the retreat. When you're working in medicine, you forget people's names. It's quite ironic. You are working through the deepest part of each other's life experiences, yet you don't know the name of the person across from you. I didn't need to know this man's name, either. All I needed was what he gave me: the acknowledgment that he understood what I was feeling and that I had to get home safely.

The anticipation of seeing Shannon and my children filled me with emotion. I got out of that car and started crying, and I gave him all the money I had. When I entered the RV, Shannon and I gave each other a hug and a kiss, and she started crying along with me. We couldn't believe how much seven days had changed our lives. We had been FaceTiming for hours a day, reflecting, talking, and sharing, so we had already gone through the apologies and the conflict resolution.

This was a moment of pure joy and reconnection as if it were the first time I had ever seen her when she stepped off the escalator at the Marriott Marquis in Times Square in New York City. I remember that day the same way I remember this moment, but the intensity was incredible because now we had known each other for 11 years. We had three children together. We had gone on these amazing journeys over the last four years. We had reinvented ourselves. We were operating from such a deeper and stronger paradigm.

This was the beginning of a very intense process. I joke about it now, but I wish I'd had caution tape around me when I got back from doing ayahuasca. I wish I had worn a shirt that said, *"Talk to me in 20 days."* This was not my circumstance, though. When you do something like this, naturally, your whole family wants to know how it went. "What did you learn? Are you okay?" When the medicine is in you, you clean, clear, and purge, so when you run into conflict, you are unfiltered.

In the 20 days after I returned to America, I had some of the most intense conversations of my life. Every single conflict that was deep in my soul was addressed with every single family member that I loved. I had to clean and clear my slate. I grew up Catholic, so confession was not a new concept for me: "Bless me, Father, for I have sinned." What I learned in ayahuasca is if you hurt anyone, you confess that to them. And I did it. It was horrible. To every person I had hurt, I confessed what I'd done to them. I am still doing this because it takes time and awareness, but for the first 20 days, I talked to everyone in my inner circle whom I needed to reconnect with. It was such a beautiful time.

We were supposed to leave Florida and return to our house in Utah, but we couldn't. I wasn't ready to drive 2,300 miles. I didn't even want to drive at night. I couldn't be in big groups of people. It was a very intimate time for my family. I share this intimacy with you because if you're planning to do this type of work, you need to take a month off after you return. I couldn't do anything other than focus on staying stable and integrating.

I'm so grateful for my assistant because she kept the wheels on the bus with my financial firm. She was talking to the clients and playing defense for me. She will hold a place in my heart for the rest of my life. She was and is my sister, but not my biological sister. I treat her like a sibling, and she treats me the same way. When you do this work, you need to prepare for what's to come after just as much as you prepare for the experience itself.

The physical side of his process is intense. If you talk to anyone who's done this type of plant medicine, many report similar experiences. I became a little clairvoyant for a while. If I talked to too many people, I might feel crazy, or they might think I am crazy. That was part of my process. I have heard this from others as well. It is why you want to be quiet and in quiet places. You don't want to be in big crowds because you're still going through your process. Being in an RV park wasn't ideal. Fortunately, the place we were at had plenty of stuff for our kids to do, and I had a large support system of friends. I'm beyond grateful for those people who were there to help me and Shannon through these 20 days.

Finally, we were ready, and we headed back to Utah. This had been our longest trip so far, 95 days. We were all ready to get out of the 410 square feet of the RV and get back to our house in Utah. We completed the trip in three days, just in time for Shannon's birthday the next day.

As we celebrated her birthday, the weather rocked my world. It was a really intense winter in Utah in 2023. It snowed almost every day in March. I could not get grounded. I couldn't come back to the center. I could not be outside enough. I said to Shannon, "Can we please go back to Costa Rica?" I think she hesitated for about 30 seconds before saying yes. She knew that it would be good for all of us. We put everything together in six days and were scheduled to go to Costa Rica for the month of April.

These four weeks were some of the most beautiful of my life because I had finally come out of the medicine. I had become aware of what I had done wrong. It is important to understand what you perceive to be wrong in your life. For me, the major "wrong" was that I had never been present. I was always multitasking and focusing on my work. I had cleared my conscience, and I was completely focused on my family. Now, we were traveling as a family on our first vacation in a decade.

The day before I left, the company that I was working for at the time told me I was not allowed to take my laptop. I smiled, called my assistant, and said, "This is amazing. I won't be allowed to work for a month." Thank goodness for her because she kept things running smoothly for the month. It was the first time since I had had a family that the only thing I did every day was wake up, meditate, journal, be with my family, be with the kids, make sure we ate healthy food, and make sure that we went to bed at a reasonable time. I felt like a newborn in a 37-year-old body: eat, sleep, go to the bathroom, feel safe.

I was able to see my kids for who they were, almost like it was the first time I'd really met them. We spent every day in nature, and we celebrated with good food. If you've been to Costa Rica, you know the food is divine.

However, I had to decide what to do professionally. The root cause of my unhappiness and disengagement with my life was my work. Shannon had been building The Motion of Gratitude for six years, and we were going to go all in on it together, which required me to make a professional pivot. In addition, the company I was working for was not going to let me work outside of the United States. We decided that Costa Rica was a very important part of our journey, and we would want to live there four to five months out of the year.

While in Costa Rica, I was introduced to my new partner at my new financial firm. We did not come to any formal deal, but the wheels were in motion for the next chapter of my professional life. We came back to America in June, and Shannon and I went all in on the new business, putting strategies in place, which I'll share more about in the last part of this section.

As I write this book, everything we planned came together, even the house we are staying in. It all happened in a serendipitous way that could only have been divinely supported. The number of things that had to go right for us to be here blows my mind. One of them makes me smile: the bracelets we wear for our company. Shannon designed what she wanted six years ago. These bracelets have a Costa Rican style, though, at the time, we had never been to Costa Rica, nor did we think it would be part of our journey. To be where we are now, doing the work we're doing, writing this book, and launching our company must be part of a bigger plan. There's no other way for me to rationalize how much it makes sense and how many synchronicities had to fall into place.

Here are a couple of other things that changed drastically for me after my ayahuasca experience. The month before we got back to Utah, we had a quarter of a cow delivered to our house, so I was eating red meat quite a bit. But after doing ayahuasca, I could no longer eat it, smell it, or go near it. I don't think there's anything wrong with red meat. I love a good steak. I just discovered that my body had to work so hard to process it, which was a big part of my health issues, why my cholesterol was high, and my blood pressure was going up. The medicine was teaching me that my behaviors were not healthy for me. I believe that all food is medicine and every human is unique. This was my awareness. I believe our diets are a process of guessing and checking. I do not have any judgment about red meat. I learned that it wasn't good for me. I also learned that I like simple foods: rice, beans, and greens. I even gave up coffee for a while.

Parts of me wanted to go back to my old way of living, but every time I did, I felt sick. I would make the kids meat for dinner and have a bite or two, but it didn't taste good. It was frustrating. Every time I tried to do what I had always done before, things that I love to do, it wouldn't serve me. I would go to people's houses, and there was nothing for me to eat. People would say, "You're a vegetarian?" and I would have to justify my new life choices.

"I'm just not eating meat right now."

"Oh, you don't drink alcohol? Is something wrong with you?"

"No, I just don't drink alcohol anymore."

In our society, people tend to judge you when you make changes. This is part of coming into knowing who you are. I was evolving, changing physically, mentally, and emotionally, and people were confused.

What other physical changes did I experience? I used to ride a road bike a hundred miles a week. I became so aware of people texting and driving that I was too scared to ride it. This had always been a reality, but now I noticed how unaware people were of me when I was on the bike. I felt like my life was in danger. I stopped trusting people with my life. This was frustrating because I had never noticed people's lack of awareness before. Because I was so aware of my surroundings, I felt unsafe doing something that I really enjoyed. So, I had to find alternatives. Hiking became my new outdoor medicine. Hiking up the mountains of Utah and looking down on the valley is an amazing paradox to explore.

Physical adaptations were required for me to come back to my center. I share the physical side of this because it will come up if you choose to explore plant medicine. I have witnessed this with so many people. It is unavoidable.

Since I've been on this journey, I have helped a lot of people integrate. People learn things about themselves that they don't want to learn, and they have to apply that learning to their current situation. They receive downloads they wish they had never gotten. You have to be ready and willing to change. If you do this type of work, you're going to be forced to change, and that is the reality of it.

On the positive side, I love yoga now. I can do yoga every day. Yoga has become the most important part of my ritual because I can physically, mentally, and spiritually work on myself all at once. I love being in nature now. I need to take my shoes off. I need to walk outside barefoot. I need to get grounded. I feel frequency. I feel energy. If I stare at a computer screen for five hours in a row, I feel like I'm going to short-circuit.

Now, I require myself to take scheduled breaks. There has to be scheduled time for me to meditate. I'm aware that when my nervous system is out of whack, and I'm parenting, I have to step away from the situation so I can control my emotions. Understanding the physical changes that we need to thrive is critical to maintaining a higher state of consciousness.

Part of the mission of The Motion of Gratitude is to empower people to live, love, and parent consciously. There's a practical side to that, the physical side. Think of what a child needs. We need to double down on behaviors that fulfill those needs, so we all feel safe. We need to drink enough water every day to be hydrated. We need to get enough sleep every night. We need to eat clean food. Every time we choose not to follow through on our needs, we drop out of higher states of consciousness.

We are still human, so we will still participate in self-destructive behavior. For example, we all fight gluten intolerance, but we still order pizza. We know that taking the kids to get gelato is going to cause an issue, but we need them to go to school that day so we can work. We fall into that trap as parents. There is no pursuit of perfection in my home, and Shannon and I certainly do not have this figured out.

Shannon and I work hard every day to be the best versions of ourselves, but we forgive ourselves when we drop to the bottom of the paradox. When we're down there, we look each other in the eyes and say, "Look at what we're doing. Let's start working our way to the top of the paradox. Let's get back to our power. Let's cross the threshold and change for tomorrow." The only way we can start the change is to take a deep breath and acknowledge it now.

As you go through the evolution of your consciousness in this type of work, the most important phrase you need to remember is: BE GENTLE.

CHAPTER 14

Emotional Shift

In this chapter, we're going to explore the emotional changes. The higher the level of your consciousness, the more you will explore. The more you explore, the more you will unravel parts of yourself that may or may not want to.

Before going to Costa Rica, I was already a highly sensitive person. In my previous professional life, we did a lot of training around EQ (emotional intelligence), a buzzphrase in corporate America for years. We all know what IQ is, but EQ is our ability to navigate and interpret situations.

This was a very beneficial side of my psyche to explore because it helped me to be a very successful financial planner. Being a highly sensitive person is a double-edged sword. I have always had a sixth sense for reading the room and understanding people's emotions and feelings. In my career as a financial planner, this allowed me to embrace those feelings and emotions, and people would open up to me because they felt safe. I was willing to explore those edges with them. I could put together a meaningful financial plan that would help them achieve their goals in a more linear fashion plan.

The negative side of being highly sensitive is that when people give me feedback, I take it to heart. Whether good or bad, it impacted me, and I would have to sit with these things for quite some time and determine how they were relevant. Well… after coming back from Costa Rica, this level of sensitivity went through the roof.

I could walk into a room, and I could feel everything. It all came through to me in frequency. I am not saying I could read anyone's mind or anything like that, but I could feel their feelings. I could look into their eyes and feel their emotions. This was a little bit destabilizing for me. For the first three weeks, I had to be very aware of who I was spending time with. I spent a lot of time in self-isolation with my family. Shannon was very supportive during this time.

I felt like the computer in my mind had been reset and now had an entirely new operating system. It was an upgrade, and it worked fast, but I had to learn how to embrace the new. I was able to process information more efficiently, and I was more aware of the circumstances around me. This was very intense emotionally, as clarity comes with strings attached. The clearer our minds become, the more unraveled the strings attached to our old self become, the self that no longer serves us. This is not an instant process. It takes a strategy and relentless patience to unwind the old versions of us to drop into the new. I am still going through this process, and it's been almost one year.

The most intense part of the process for me is how every single emotion I have now is heightened, as are my five senses. I had not cried for years, but now I find myself getting into emotional states on a daily basis. For example, I get emotional now when I watch the sun come up. I'm grateful for the morning. This is a very beautiful part of me because it is one that I had not previously experienced.

There is a negative side, though. I am a very intense person. I have very high standards, and with those standards, sometimes, if the kids are not listening and I've asked them to do something ten times, I will get frustrated and angry. That emotion is also heightened. This is a double-edged sword that I have to navigate when doing this type of work. Dealing with these heightened senses will be a lifelong journey.

I hope I maintain this level of awareness. I would much rather live with these heightened emotions than the numbness I felt before. When I was playing the money game full time, I was able to numb parts of myself in the pursuit of worldly success. Now that I am playing the human game full time, I enjoy the feeling. I enjoy experiencing the beauty of the world and slowing down. There are days I wish I could not feel everything, but that is usually when I am out of alignment.

The next focus for me was how to stabilize every morning. Prior to my ayahuasca experience, I had been firmly on the river. I had meditated and journaled but had fallen away from my practices. I believe that if I hadn't, I would not have had such a dramatic experience with the ayahuasca. But I had gotten into the rhythm of waking up, looking at my email, checking the news, drinking a cup of coffee, and waiting for the day to happen to me instead of for me.

If you are feeling this way, it is a key indicator that you are slipping away from these higher states of consciousness. As always, acknowledge it, be gentle, forgive yourself, and re-engage with your meditation and journaling practices. Going over the waterfall of ayahuasca was very intense because I had disengaged from the practices I had been doing on a daily basis. When I got back, returning to them was critical.

Without doing our process in The Motion of Gratitude, I would have been completely destabilized. I would wake up every morning around 4 a.m. with high cortisol levels, in fight-or-flight mode—some people call it the witching hour. I would be nervous, scared, and frustrated. If I had just gotten out of bed and gone along with my day in that state of consciousness, it would have been very, very unhealthy for me.

So, I retrained my morning routine. I drank a glass of water, and then I dropped into meditation for 30 minutes. Now, if you're hearing 30 minutes and you're like, "Oh, man, I don't know how I can meditate for six minutes, let alone 30," start with two minutes. Start with three minutes. Don't jump right into a 30-minute meditation. Studies have shown that the average human cannot even consider doing a 30-minute meditation to start with, so they often end up not starting at all.

I was already meditating quite a bit. I would set an intention for each meditation, which is critical for me to be in a good state each day. Every morning, when I wake up, I still set an intention for the day. If it's a weekend, I might set an intention like, "Help me to be present, kind, and playful with my children all day." If it's a workday and I have nine meetings, "Help me to be locked into these engagements and present for each one of these people so we can do good work together." These are just examples, but it was important during this phase of my life to set an intention every morning.

I would meditate and write five things I was grateful for. Then I would go for a walk with our dog, Dublin, before sunrise. This was the most important walk of my integration. Watching the sun come up every morning allowed me to re-engage with the moment of the fourth night of the ceremony when I was terrified. It allowed me to manage my feelings and realize that they were part of a psychological lesson but not my reality. It might have been a traumatizing experience, but I learned that I needed to wake up and couldn't continue to live the life I was living. Going on this morning walk helped me to be grateful for the day and know that I am alive, I am here, and I don't have to live in that past moment.

As you read this, you are probably saying, "Well, how does this apply to me? I didn't do ayahuasca." Other life experiences can lead to this type of spiritual opening or opening to higher states of consciousness, whatever you want to call it. If you recently went through a death in the family, this is going to open up your heart. If you are currently battling a disease, have recently gone through cancer, or are working through a situation with your child that's destabilizing your relationship, it's important to realize that such moments serve as wake-up calls.

Your wake-up call might be very different from mine. It might even have happened by accident. Whatever your circumstances, having these tools to integrate those higher levels of feelings and emotions is critical because we have to breathe into this moment. The only thing that matters is this moment. Living too much in the past creates depression, and focusing too much on the future creates anxiety.

The next two things I had to focus on were love and kindness. If you have done plant medicine, this will make total sense to you because most of these medicines take you to the exact same spot where we are all connected. How we treat each other is critical as it is how we treat ourselves. We're all direct representations of how we go out into the world and walk. Everything is a mirror.

I had to re-engage in every aspect of my life with the people I was sitting with. As a financial planner, I was turning people into numbers. Any salespeople out there will be able to relate to this. You track a pipeline. You track opportunities. You set goals. You write them down. As a financial planner, if you set a goal to roll over $10 million a year, you will start to track that $833,000 a month. Then, you will go back to where it comes from, who has assets, and what you must do to capture them. This type of linear thinking became part of my reality and bled over into all aspects of my life. Sadly, if the person across from me wasn't creating a return on time, I would begin to disengage. It is sad to write this, but the acknowledgment has helped me move forward and not treat people like this ever again.

Love and kindness lead my way. With every single person I talk to every single day, I believe that I'm meant to be in that moment for a reason. It might be for me, or it might be for them; it does not matter. This reframing of relationships has been incredibly valuable for me to keep spreading good, and I have learned that one smile could change someone's entire day.

Another challenging part of this process for me was that the more aware I became, the more empathetic I became, and the more I noticed things that were destabilizing in our culture and society. I used to have a heart that was very aware of charity and doing good, but it was more of checking a box than anything else. I knew it was important to give money to those in need, feed the hungry, or help children, but it was always about me making money so I could afford to do it.

This has been entirely reframed in my mind. My purpose now is to help people. And my heart is one hundred percent engaged in helping the youth of the world. The return on equity for helping the youth of the world is zero more often than not. Obviously, you can build businesses and make things, but the intention is to help children. But we need to understand that we're at a point in history when children are very destabilized. Children today are often glued to a screen and are growing up too fast. They have access to information that I didn't get access to until I was in high school and even in college.

My purpose every morning when I wake up now is very other-focused, but only after I do the things that I need to do to stabilize my nervous system and mental health. The old version of me, however, would look at my calendar each morning, evaluate each opportunity, look at the return on equity of my meetings, and determine how I would go into each of those engagements. What I'm trying to share with you is this was a very calculated approach to my entire life, and it worked. It was working very well to build a version of me with a nice house, nice cars, and a nice income.

Today, when I wake up, I ask myself, *How am I going to love and serve?* This was a very hard process for me. I had been living out those paradoxes. I had been feeling all the feelings, for example, the boat. I have had a dream of buying a boat since I was 12 years old. I bought the boat, and I realized it wasn't the right time in my life to have it because it was pulling me away from my family. When I sold the boat, I did it intuitively. But now I had to circle back on that paradox, and I had to explore it emotionally.

I had to feel all the feelings. I had to sit in the feeling of what if this thing was not good for my marriage for all of these reasons? And how was I making Shannon feel by choosing to do this? This was a very different type of thinking. I had to think about alcohol. I had been drinking alcohol since I was 18 years old, using it as a coping mechanism because I'm a highly sensitive person. I had to think about the feelings that I was creating inside of my home. I would work all day, and if I couldn't manage my stress at the end of the day because I was so tired, I would use alcohol to do it. Then I would become tired, and I wouldn't engage with my kids and my wife at the end of the day. Or I would become a fun dad on the weekends and unwind all of the hard work that Shannon was doing during the week while homeschooling our children. I had to explore these paradoxes from Shannon's point of view. I had to explore them with my children. This is part of the process.

When we are living an unconscious life, it is easy to justify our decisions. A simple example is alcohol. And I'm not attacking anyone who drinks alcohol; I'm just using it because it is an example from my life. I was unconsciously drinking alcohol to manage and justify my feelings: "Oh, I might have a little bit of a temper today, but that's because I'm hungover." "Oh, I have to do [XYZ] because I forgot to do something yesterday because I had a good buzz." I was constantly living in this cycle of justifying my behavior so that I could cope with my feelings.

When you go through one of these wake-up calls and you step into a higher state of consciousness—those are the words I like to use—you're on the other side of this paradox. At that point, everything you used to do seems silly. So, now I don't drink alcohol. Now, I'm on this side of the conscious paradox.

Not drinking alcohol allows me to stay focused when it comes to the food I eat, both at night and in the morning. I'm not hungover, so that frees me up to be more engaged in my exercise routine on the weekends. I am more present with my children, and I'm in my body psychologically. I can still have fun with my kids without having a substance inside of me.

Here are warning signs to help you spot unconscious behavior. You do something, and your first thought the next day is, *I wish I hadn't done that.* Or you go out to lunch and get food, and 30 minutes later, you feel sick or tired. These are red flags that you're currently doing things from an unconscious point of view. It's okay. Step one is acknowledgment. Step two, you might laugh at yourself. I think adding levity helps you be gentler on yourself. Through gentleness, you will begin the changing process.

The process will be hard, and you will fall back into your familiar. However, every time you fall back, you will start to speed up the process. The goal is to not avoid your familiar. The goal is to bounce back as quickly as you can. For me, with alcohol, this took 18 months. Some days, I felt like I had amnesia. I would have a really hard day at work and then think, *Oh, I'm going to have a couple of beers.* Then I wouldn't feel good, I would eat fried food, and the cycle would start again. I'd wake up the next morning thinking, *Oh, I wish I hadn't done that.*

Going through these states of evolution is a process, and accountability is critical. I've been blessed to have my wife as an amazing accountability partner for this. We have very good communication in our marriage, and we're very good at forgiving each other for doing the things that we know are self-sabotaging. Sometimes, we yell at each other, but more often than not, we laugh and say, "Hey, you're doing it again." If you don't have this in your marriage or relationship, this is where coaches can be really helpful. I have hired coaches my whole life.

I started to go to a therapist when I was nine years old because of my parents' divorce. They have always been a critical part of my story. If you find someone you can trust and let them in, you can be vulnerable. And the more vulnerable you are, the more you can move forward with this process. The other thing that was critical for my emotional state, which we talked a little about in the last chapter, was the physical changes. Your environment is such a critical indicator of your entire life. There are things about me that I am so clear about now that are annoying but true. Let me give you an example.

I struggle with seasonal sadness. That is my truth. I grew up in Pennsylvania, and every winter, the lack of sunlight affected my personality. I would gain weight, drink more alcohol, and go outside less often. Now, I like being a migratory human. I like migrating to warmer climates. I miss the seasons, but it helps me maintain a higher state of consciousness. We homeschool our children—or world-school them, depending on where we are at. When we were homeschooling our children in Utah and Pennsylvania and were stuck inside the house twenty-four hours a day, it was very destabilizing for us. Your environment will impact your emotions. It's unavoidable. So, if you have the luxury of breathing into a migratory pattern, consider it for your family. I know it's not easy, especially if you have kids, but depending on your circumstances, the benefits might outweigh the challenges.

If you can't migrate, there are other things you could do anywhere in the world that will help you with this. Technology has come so far. I have an infrared sauna. There are grounding mats. Significant research has been done on techniques and strategies to help manage seasonal sadness, seasonal depression, or whatever you might call it.

We live in a very beautiful time in history where we have seemingly endless access to information. If there's something in your life that's impacting you emotionally, find someone who is an expert in that field and embrace them. I have given my life work now to gratitude. I know no matter where I am in the world, if I do not start my day with gratitude, I do not start it on the right foot. I have to write five things I'm grateful for. I have to meditate. The more I do, the more I need my tools.

The last thing that I would encourage everyone to do when it comes to managing their emotional state is to journal. You can write five things you're grateful for every day. That takes about three or four minutes. Our brains think so many thoughts. Some studies say 72,000 thoughts a day, some say 50,000. We don't have to identify a number, but we know that thoughts are constantly racing inside our brains. Writing a negative thought down helps to purge it. If it's a positive thought, writing it down can bring it to life. I look at my journals all the time.

Journaling has been one of the most effective tools I've used on my alcohol journey. I always knew that it took 12 days for me to stabilize emotionally. Again, I would get amnesia. I would choose to give it up again, and on day nine, I would have a short fuse, and I'd get grumpy, and I'd be unable to control my nervous system. I could go back to my journal and say, "Oh, yeah, this is your process." Be gentle. Don't hold yourself to too high of a standard. Putting your thoughts down in a journal creates a shortcut through your process. Save all of your journals. Put them somewhere safe. That way, if you're going through something very hard in your life right now, as you start to document it, you'll have a catalog for your brain on paper.

Life works in cycles. Journaling allows you to go back and remind yourself what you did and thought before. The younger we are, the more energy we tend to have. When looking at notes from five years ago, you might find that you ran headfirst into the problem back then. Wisdom is created through knowledge. Create your own wisdom. Now, you're the older version of yourself, who may not have as much time or energy. You may have gone through that lesson before you had kids, but now you have them. You don't have as much time to focus on the problem and the solution. So you can create your own shortcuts.

Reading other books can also help you create shortcuts. Whoever you surround yourself with and whatever you read is who you become. I firmly believe this. I learned this when I was 16 years old, and it's been the most stable truth of my existence. So, to expedite your cycles, read what you wrote in your journal and then add to that the insight gained from other people. The goal is not to avoid the cycle; it's to move through it more efficiently with ease, love, and kindness.

CHAPTER 15

The Present Moment

I want to pull you into the present moment. I led with vision, and then we explored my paradoxes. I shared all the things I had to explore and deconstruct to go up my first mountain. I chased the unicorn up the mountain, which, for me, was money. In the middle of the book, you saw me go down into the valley. You have to descend to ascend the next mountain. This part of the book is my second mountain. This is why I wake up. This is my Gratosis. The only thing I think about is sovereignty. Your definition of Gratosis is unique to you. You must identify your second mountain. We must use all the lessons from our first mountain to thrive on the second.

Why sovereignty? What sovereignty means to me is the freedom to operate. I do the things that I love on a daily basis and provide for my family with abundance. I take care of others and, in the process, take care of my family. I was blessed to take care of people on my first mountain, but the money box defined me. The people who hire a financial planner generally have two main triggers: fear and money. People hire a professional because they fear the financial markets and whether they have a good plan.

I co-founded a company called The Motion of Gratitude with Shannon. One of my main triggers is when my kids are not grateful. I believe that if I can do a really good job as a father teaching my children to be grateful, I can teach the world because the hardest lesson that I've learned is how to be a father and be grateful. And it will never end as I walk on this planet.

The second mountain, for me, is so clear, and it is so much bigger than the first. The hard part is going down into that valley. I really care about my clients. I was a financial planner for 18 years. I am not the kind of financial planner who can just ride off into the sunset and sell my book on business. That was never an option for me. I had made promises to these people because I thought that this was going to be my life's work. I made a pivot, and it was my responsibility to make sure that my clients landed somewhere safe, with people who cared as much about them as I did.

I had to leave the corporate America financial planning channel. This was not easy. I had to pay off what's called a forgivable note with the transition. There was no financial windfall. Everything came from my heart. Choosing to climb my second mountain has not been easy. We don't start over, though. We upgrade. I knew it had to happen, but I didn't know how it was going to happen. I knew I had to become an independent financial planner because that was the only way I could have sovereignty. I knew I wanted my clients to be with fiduciaries. I knew I didn't want any corporate agenda coming down into their financial plan for the products that they had to purchase.

I knew what I wanted, but I didn't know where to go. This is where trust and surrender are beautiful truths. The only way this could have happened for me was with God as the wind in my sails. When my family and I came back to Costa Rica in April of 2023, I was introduced to a man who is now my business partner. The day I met this gentleman, I was sitting on a property, and there was this beautiful white German Shepherd. Her name is Onyx. Her job on this farm is to protect the livestock. She had two pups and walked the property all night long.

When I was introduced to my new firm, I did not Google my partner because I didn't want to have any preconceived notions going into our phone call. I wanted the interaction to be a hundred percent instinctual. The name of my firm has the word Onyx in it. Black onyx has been used for thousands of years to block fear. Now I had a white dog named Onyx in front of me. I smiled at the paradox. I chuckled and embraced the divine comedy, using it as the first breadcrumb to make this transition. I know it might sound silly, but you have to be aware that the divine comedy is playing out in your life every day. This was the beginning of one of the most powerful relationships that I currently have in my life.

This gentleman paved the way for me to write my ticket to get out of the financial planning business day to day and take care of my clients. His team loves people as much as I love them. I know that my clients are safe. I know that our team will care for them as much as I did. You do not have to blow up your past as you go down the mountain. You don't have to put dynamite on the first mountain. Be a bridge. Build a bridge from the top of that mountain to the middle of the next mountain. Get creative. The more you meditate, the more you journal about your gratitude, and the more you write, the more creative solutions will pop into your psyche. Though I didn't want to look at a trade blotter ever again, I wasn't going to turn my back on these people. And I didn't have to.

Staying with the previous firm wasn't an option. By June of 2023, I had decided that leaving was my only choice. I had to transfer my clients again in the summer of 2023. This is not a fun process for anyone. You can't take information with you to your new firm. There is more inconvenience for the clients than there should be because the firm owns the information that they shared with you. So, you have to restart.

Think of getting a new doctor. The doctor doesn't know you, so they have to build the client file. Well, this was a little more frustrating because I knew my clients, but I couldn't keep all of their data, so I had to collect everything all over again. This was easier than the first time because the relationship was there, but it was still annoying for everyone. Not to mention, in 2023, there were all kinds of technology issues, and people had to get to know new software packages and new platforms. I'm grateful that I was able to secure a good place for my clients with people who love them and care about their financial plans.

I did not put dynamite on my first mountain. I did not start over. I used all the knowledge that I had acquired over the 18 years to build a business in the financial sector. Now, this was all a process, a transition. I thought I was going to be a financial planner for two more years. I thought I was going to have time to converse with clients and share a gradual transition to the new team. But sometimes, you're going to get winks or nudges from the universe or God, who says, "That's not an option." For me, that kept coming through on a very consistent basis. I kept feeling that I was no longer aligned, and the more I pretended to be patient with the transition, the less genuine I was becoming.

Everything sped up. In October of 2023, in a deep meditation, I realized that I needed to stop being a financial planner every day. It hit me like a wall, and I started crying. Any time you make a massive pivot, there is going to be a mourning process. I came downstairs, still crying, and Shannon asked me, "What's wrong? What happened?"

We went out on the back porch, where I looked her in the eye and said, "I can't do it anymore. I cannot be a financial planner. I cannot do this every day. I cannot pretend that these people's financial plans are the most important thing in my life. It's not fair for me, and it's certainly not fair for them."

Shannon, in shock, hesitated for about 30 seconds. Then she looked me in the eye and said, "We will figure it out."

I called my partner the next day and shared the news with him. His first response was to congratulate me. God stacked the deck for me. He is also stacking the deck for you. We can choose to operate in this level of faith, and it will block fear. It doesn't mean that it's easy to make these decisions. I had dedicated 18 years of my life to being a financial planner. I had done all of the classes, including CFP, CLU, CHFC, CASL, and licenses. Being a financial planner had become my identity. It was who I was. People would ask me all the time, "What do you do?" and I would answer, "I help create financial freedom for people as they define it." It was who I was. And now I was saying, "I don't want to be that person anymore. I want to step fully into The Motion of Gratitude. I want to sell gratitude for the rest of my life."

It is critical in these moments of clarity that you sit in them and know that they're happening for you and not to you. Understand that the experience will be intense. I'm glad I had the bridge built between my first and second mountains, but as I have walked across the bridge, sometimes there's a missing board, and sometimes I slip.

That is part of the process. In the last chapter, I mentioned that we had planned to come to Costa Rica on November 1. We had booked the trip before I made this decision. This was already part of my negotiations with my new partner. He knew that I was going to be in Costa Rica for five months. That was part of the reason I had to go independent. My second mountain is sovereignty, and we had to get creative on how to get there.

If you're going to be outside of the US for five months, you need to work on a team because people in the United States have to do your trading. Teams are the only option for this lifestyle. What was going to be a trip to the jungle for the winter to celebrate the transition, integration, and migration of all of my clients to my new platform became the cocooning process for the butterfly to come out of The Motion of Gratitude. The process of being in Costa Rica for five months is all about who we want to become.

I still go into my past life for shortcuts. I look at my journal notes. I reflect on all the things I had to learn to get to this moment. I have thousands of relationships because of my financial planning journey, and I'm so grateful that those people are supportive and excited about this next level of my life. Your past has created this present moment. Do not spend too much time there. Without a vision, you will get confused. We have to have a vision. We have to know what we want and where we are going.

However, I can't just sit outside, look up at the stars, and say, "I'm going to manifest this reality." It doesn't work that way. The manifestation is in the work. It's in the doing that we create. I opened this book with my vision of when I will be a hundred years old. I might not live to be a hundred, but every day, I wake up knowing that I am here for a reason. Visions are critical, and over the last three years, I stopped writing them. When I fell into the sadness of my darkness, I stopped doing the things I'd always done to get to where I was going. I was self-sabotaging my life because I was unclear what I wanted. Visions create excitement. Excitement creates behaviors, and behaviors create results. We win in the DOING! We have to know what our second mountain is. I might have a third mountain in this life. I will figure that out after I climb this one!

If you've ever climbed a mountain, you know that it takes a massive amount of resilience, and you often want to give up. More often than not, if I get blisters when climbing a mountain, it's on the descent. When my toes hit the front of my shoes, that's when my feet hurt. Coming down your first mountain will cause sore feet. There's pressure in the descent, but there's joy in the ascent. As you're climbing your second mountain, you have to pause and breathe. The higher you go, the more you have to breathe.

This metaphor is so perfect for your walk in life. You have to have a vision, and the higher you go, the more breathwork you have to do. The more you have to breathe, the more you have to journal, the more you have to be grateful. You have to double down on the tools to go higher. And you have to surround yourself with people who are going to support you and build you up. They are hiking right next to you up this mountain. I promise the people next to you are going through the same struggles; they just look different. When I go hiking up big mountains, I don't go alone.

The higher you go, the steeper the mountains are, and the more you risk. Now, don't be confused. I'm not a mountain climber. The highest mountain I've climbed is Mount Timpanogos in Utah, which is 11,753 feet. I am scared of heights. I wanted to give up climbing that mountain, but because I was with a friend who is not scared of heights, I got to the top. I stood on top of that mountain for three minutes with my knees shaking, terrified, but I did it.

Shannon and I are passionate about helping people "Feel the Impact." of an intentional gratitude practice and being present in the moment. We can learn from our past for our future, but the only thing that matters is the current breath. The more we breathe into this current moment, the more we drop into the state of flow, a beautiful state of serendipity where you see the miracle of life in your surroundings. You see the miracle of the universe. The more you see miracles, the more they will come into your life. Miracles will appear everywhere. You just have to find them.

Do random acts of kindness today. Your miracle for someone might be buying them a sandwich. Your miracle for someone might be going to a food bank and helping prepare food. Your miracle might be that your teenage neighbor is going through a hard time, so you go and play basketball with them. That one moment might give that young person hope.

The things that are happening in our world right now are sad. We have more teen suicides than in the history of humanity. The darkness that these young people are facing stems from unconscious behavior. These are things that we did not have to address in our youth, my youth. I did not have an iPhone. I did not have social media. I rode my bike every day. Physical movement was the most prevalent part of my day as a young teen. We would ride our bikes around and play in the woods or play basketball at the playground. Life was simpler. And if my friends didn't tell me that they were going to hang out, I didn't know that I was left out. Having that naive reality was critical for me as a highly sensitive child. Children today don't have that luxury. When kids are rejected, they see it on social media. We are in a time of feelings. Feelings matter right now. We need to all get better at embracing the real truth of feelings.

And as I go into my future, I want people to embrace a conversation about feelings. We all want to feel safe. We all want to have good food to survive. We need to drink water. The things that make us happy are not as intense as what has become the reality for our society. We don't need nicer cars. We don't need bigger houses. We need good food and enough water. We need to feel safe talking to others. We need to be able to express our feelings. We need to be heard. And we have to stop rejecting people for their belief systems.

We all have our own unique walk, our own unique journey. We all have been through things that other people don't know about. We need to explore a path to relationships that minimizes judgment. If we don't, we will hurt people by accident. We also need to be able to disagree, but it is critical that we hug at the end of a disagreement.

There is so much division in the world right now: politics, gender issues, racism, war. We're all not going to get along. That's not the goal. The goal is that we each find our community and stop self-isolating. When you find your tribe, don't say that it is better than another. That is old thinking. Admire the tribe. See the beauty in them and respect them. Just because that other tribe over there votes one way or believes one thing doesn't mean that the tribe has to force you to vote and believe that way. Just accept one another. Surrender to the beauty of the inconsistency around the life that we all live. If we all got along about everything, life would not be fun. We like adventures. We like amusement parks. We are all here to learn lessons. We are all here to understand conflict, and we are certainly all here to have fun. The human game is a beautiful one.

The money game is part of it. My first mountain revolved totally around the money game. I thought, one day, I would wake up and have financial freedom, and then I would live. The human game: every day, I wake up, and I live. We are at a beautiful time in history where we're all starting to understand human psychology better, differently, and in a more productive way.

If you wake up today and go through the motions, doing what you've always done, getting the same result that you don't want, and this disturbs you, congratulations. You've come into a heightened state of consciousness. The awareness is the beauty of the solution.

Other programs out there cost thousands and thousands of dollars. The average income in the United States is under $50,000. People can't afford to take 20% of their income to elevate themselves. Credit card debt is at an all-time high, so that's not a resource to draw on. Our goal is to teach people to come through a spiritual opening for $48. We want people to spend less than a tank of gas to start elevating their loving-kindness practice. I pray every day that Gratosis becomes a mainstream diagnosis.

I would like to end this journey in the same way we started it. Vision is everything. If we never cross paths again, please do ONE thing from reading this book. Get out a piece of paper. Pick a meaningful future date. When I started vision planning, I always used January 1st for the next year, and I would write my vision around Thanksgiving.

Today is January 1st..........

THANK YOU FOR READING MY BOOK!

Here are a few free bonus resources.

I appreciate your interest in my book and value your feedback as it helps me improve future versions of this book. I would appreciate it if you could leave your invaluable review on Amazon.com with your feedback. Thank you!

Made in the USA
Columbia, SC
29 April 2024

521439e2-143b-4e45-b98a-823b32f19199R01